More Praise for
A Field Guide for the Missional Congregation

"Rick Rouse and Craig Van Gelder have produced a field guide to help congregations on their quest of participating in the mission of God. The book does not focus on leaders, but rather on what makes for light and life in congregations. The book would serve a staff or congregational council well in either ongoing study through a year or as a road map for a retreat. The seven keys open conversations and share wisdom for congregational leaders to deepen missional focus and navigate through tension and change. This book will help congregations that seek to grow more deeply fruitful and faithful in Christ's mission."

Jon Anderson, Bishop,
Southwestern Minnesota Synod ELCA

"I have used field guides for many years to help identify plants and animals in the wilderness. The best of these books clearly describe the species on the printed page so it then can be readily identified in the field. Rouse and Van Gelder's book applies this principle in terms of the marks of God's mission and the identity of the congregation. The result is a clear, practical, and helpful resource for congregational leaders. I highly recommend its use."

Gary M. Wollersheim, Bishop,
Northern Illinois Synod ELCA

"Change is not an idea—and neither is mission. The Church is being called to a new season of missional power and this book will help you to join this Spirit-led movement."

Michael Foss, Senior Pastor,
Lutheran Church of the Redeemer, Atlanta, Georgia
Author of Power Surge and Real Faith for Real Life

"Rouse and Van Gelder offer experienced and practical insights for any of us who seek to lead congregations away from maintaining members to growing Christ-followers. This field guide can assist lay and clergy leaders on the eternal quest of living out the great commandment and the great commission."

Stephen S. Talmage, Bishop,
Grand Canyon Synod ELCA

"Rouse and Van Gelder harvest in this field guide delicious, mature fruit sown from the seeds of those laboring to re-form the church as a missional community. This articulation of best practices is solidly grounded in the soil of Trinitarian theology. It should serve as a practical and usable guide for congregational leaders committed to cultivating their own field as God's fruitful vineyard in mission."

Craig Nessan,
Wartburg Theological Seminary, Dubuque, Iowa

"This book invites congregations on a quest. But, be careful! This quest guide isn't a how-to book with easy steps for success; it is a book about releasing a congregation's energy for creative change and cultivating an imagination for mission. Congregations that are ready for this journey will want to keep this field guide handy."

Richard Bliese, President,
Luther Seminary, St. Paul, Minnesota

"Much of the current literature that is part of the missional church conversation remains at a theoretical level. With this field guide, Rouse and Van Gelder have produced an excellent and accessible resource for congregational leadership teams seeking to create dynamic, healthy ministries that more fully and effectively participate in God's mission to heal the world."

Michael Peck, Senior Pastor,
Holy Cross Lutheran Church, Overland Park, Kansas

"Rick Rouse and Craig Van Gelder have written a biblically grounded and theologically savvy book that makes the strong case that the church itself is inherently missional. Loaded with a great deal of reality and case studies, this book is an invaluable field guide for pastors and leaders.

Rick Barger, Lead Pastor,
Abiding Hope Lutheran Church, Littleton, Colorado
Founder of the Academy for Adaptive Leadership and Spiritual Formation

"A map, a compass, good boots, and food for the journey of witnessing the Spirit's wonders. Transformational keys are landmarks, vignettes the travelogues, and practical prose the reading of signs. Exploration, discovery, new sights at every turn mark the venture; and this guide interprets the way."

Christopher E. Hagen, Interim Pastor,
Minneapolis Area Synod ELCA

"Rouse and Van Gelder make a clear statement about what it means to be a missional congregation and provide a helpful road map for the journey to becoming one. Leaders of congregations that are serious about transformation would be well served to explore this field guide together to gain a shared understanding of both the imperatives and the perils of the heavy lifting involved in transformation."

Alan Walter, Parish Ministry Associate/Licensed Lay Minister,
Central States Synod ELCA

A **FIELD GUIDE**
FOR THE
MISSIONAL
CONGREGATION

Embarking on a Journey of Transformation

Rick Rouse and Craig Van Gelder

Augsburg Fortress
Minneapolis

We dedicate this volume to our wives,
Beth Lewis and Barbara Van Gelder,
for their ongoing encouragement, support, and love.
We would not want to embark on any quest
without them!

Purchases of ten or more copies of this book are available at a discount from the publisher. For more information, contact the sales department at Augsburg Fortress, Publishers, 1-800-328-4648, or write to: Sales Director, Augsburg Fortress, Publishers, Box 1209, Minneapolis, MN 55440-1209.

Artist: Julia Jaakala
Additional art: Micah Thompson; Cover map: *Ancient Maps*, Planet Art
Cover design/photography: D. M. Running
Book design: Eileen Z. Engebretson

Library of Congress Cataloging-in-Publication Data
Rouse, Richard W.
  A field guide for the missional congregation : embarking on a journey of transformation / Rick Rouse and Craig Van Gelder.
    p. cm.
  ISBN 978-0-8066-8044-6 (alk. paper)
  1. Mission of the church. 2. Church renewal—Lutheran Church. 3. Church growth—Lutheran Church. I. Van Gelder, Craig. II. Title.
  BV601.8.R685 2008
   253.088'284135—dc22   2008000150

The paper used in this publication meets the minimum requirements of American National Standard for Information Sciences—Permanence of Paper for Printed Library Materials, ANSI Z329.48-1984.

Manufactured in the U.S.A.
12   11   10   09   08   3   4   5   6   7   8   9   10

Contents

Seven Transformational Keys

Foreword

While I have not been a parish minister for decades, I have been involved in congregational life sufficiently to stay alert to the problems and possibilities of the local church in its connections with the church as the Body of Christ. With that background in mind, I read this book with one special interest. So many guides and manuals for church life are slightly churchified versions of what one can get on the cheap (I am not talking about money, but about mind-stretching) from administrative counsel for businesses. We do not need one more of them.

Instead, I looked for the theological motifs, backgrounds, inspirations, and intentions that in our present situation mean the biblical framework. Again and again, I would pause to check out scriptural references. I am happy to say, what you will find is that the scriptural sources are the main resources, and all the talk about "missional" grows out of them. These sources are available to be put to work in congregations that are ready for transformation with this field guide to guide them.

Congregations never had it so good.

Congregations never had it so bad.

Rick Rouse and Craig Van Gelder show that they know that both of these propositions are true, or can be true, depending on what we are noticing and asking about congregations. Not only do they *know* something about both, they want to *do* something. They want to help people in local congregations have it "good," so that they can better reflect the kingdom of God.

To make sense of all this, let's examine the two propositions. "Congregations never had it so good/bad." First of all, "never" is a long time.

We can interpret the phrase here to simply mean, "when we compare congregations of today with what we are told about those of yesterday."

The second word that needs attention is "congregation," the key noun in this book's title. It represents the local church, the gathering of God's people in a particular place. These people are to be on the front line representing the kingdom of God—the sovereign, saving activity of God in Christ. Rouse and Van Gelder are not oblivious to the fact that congregations are themselves local presences of the one holy, catholic, and apostolic church, yet these two put their energies where most of us place a good deal of ours, in the local setting.

The third "word" is divided in two: "good" and "bad." Congregations never had it so good because they represent the main form of Christian expression. Remote bureaucracies, impersonal organizations, unresponsive agencies, and even experimental movements supplement, or try to supplement, what local churches do. While many of these other forms are in trouble today, by contrast, "local congregations never had it so good," and they merit attention.

This book tells how believers can help realize a "good" congregation. It is to be "missional" in being caught up in the activity of the kingdom. Our two authors show how congregations, as foretasters of the feasts to come in the realized kingdom of God, can become better at what missional activity means: the baptized are daily "born again" through repentance and the experience of forgiveness; hungry people crowd the Lord's Table and, being satisfied, are inspired to invite others; people bear each other's burdens and welcome guests to join them.

A "bad" congregation is the opposite of what we have just described. Now, congregations never had it so bad. Today many people want to be "spiritual" without being "religious" or to be "religious" without being "churched," so thought about the "kingdom" is well beyond their imagination. Many people who say they love Jesus want to go on their own and make up their responses as they go along, avoiding the company of fellow sojourners. Congregations never had it so bad because distractions in society, thanks to mass media, commerce, and ideology, impinge ever more on congregations.

Why make so much of community and congregation, as Rouse and Van Gelder do? I'd like to put it in shocking terms: we have to and get to care so much about them because they are a form in which Christ exists. The main form of God in Christ's presence among us between Jesus' ascension and coming again is the congregation. "Where two or three are gathered together in my name, there am I in the midst of them." What a challenging thing it is today to have a leadership role in a congregation. It is easy for leaders, lay and clergy, to be defeated, turn sluggish, or fade, and thus fail to experience Christ present as a congregation. Yet the promise of God is that where there is such a challenge, Christ will be present. Where there is challenge, the Holy Spirit will help us meet it.

Here is where the "missional" concept as used by these authors comes in. Whoever thinks that a short definition might suffice for this word will find his or her whole world enlarged by reading all that the concept of *missional* can mean for Christians. Something has begun to happen in these thirty years, and books like this one and projects described in it will produce more happenings. Pastor Rouse and Professor Van Gelder are not here to promote a faddish use of a term, to sell gimmicks, to peddle "Seven Easy Steps" of anything, though I am pleased to see that they offer seven—a holy number!— "Transformational Keys." They know that congregational leaders who try to unlock opportunities with these keys will meet resistance. Some local churches have locks that appear jammed or rusty or resistant for a simple reason—all these keys are calls to change. The keys in this book promise the "better" that comes when resistance to change gets resisted and people in local churches experience freedom in Christ, the Christ who exists in and *as* their transformed congregation.

Martin E. Marty

Fairfax M. Cone Distinguished Service Professor Emeritus

The University of Chicago

Introduction

Encountering God's Work Among Us: A Journey of Discovery

Did you know there is a difference between an adventure and a quest? An adventure is a journey that is taken to a particular place, all the time knowing you will safely return home in the end. A quest is something you have to do, a journey you feel compelled to take—not knowing for certain where it may lead or being sure how you are going to get there, but knowing that it is something you must pursue. We invite you to embark on a quest for becoming a missional church, exploring creatively how to participate more fully in God's mission in the world as the Spirit leads your congregation into those places, yet to be discerned, where your congregation needs to go.

Why This Book?
We believe that many pastors and lay leaders recognize the need for change in their congregations. We also believe many are looking for practical help in understanding how God might work to transform their communities of faith. In our work with pastors in the Congregational Mission and Leadership Doctor of Ministry program at Luther Seminary, we have discovered an eagerness among participating pastors to assist congregations in being more faithful participants in God's mission in the world. At the same time, our students have

indicated that there is much work to be done if attitudes are to be changed in order for this transformation to happen. This is evidenced by the results of a survey on missional leadership conducted with the pastors participating in the doctoral program at Luther Seminary. A sampling of these results includes the following:

I believe that our congregation is more comfortable with a model of ministry that primarily serves our own members rather than actively engaging the community around us in seeking to participate more fully in God's mission in the world.
82 percent agreed with this statement.

I think that my congregation needs to find a better balance between an inward ministry of serving our members and an outward ministry of discerning and participating in God's mission with our larger community.
91 percent agreed with this statement.

I "buy" into the idea of being a missional church, but find that I need some practical help in leading my congregation in trying to discern how to better participate in God's mission by becoming as much outward as inward oriented.
82 percent agreed with this statement.

I think that the members of my congregation are still somewhat resistant to a missional approach because this would require changing the way we understand our identity as the basis of how we do ministry.
70 percent agreed with this statement.

How to Use This Book

This is not a "how to" book in the popular sense of the word. It is rather a journey of exploration. It is for this reason that we are referring to it as *A Field Guide for the Missional Congregation*. The particular path each congregation must take is yet to be discovered. There are, however, clear transformational keys that can be discerned regarding how God works within congregations, and through congregations within the world. We believe that understanding these keys is foundational for pursuing the quest of becoming a missional congregation.

This field guide is designed to help cultivate a biblical and theological imagination in your congregation about how God desires to be at work among you. The intent is to help release the creative energy of God's people in today's church and within your congregation. Its focus is on helping lay leaders and church staff take this journey together as they engage the *Discovery Questions* provided at the end of each chapter. The illustrations in this book usually refer to medium-to-larger size congregations. But we firmly believe that the transformational keys that are presented apply equally well to congregations of all sizes, and also to all ministry contexts, whether they be rural, urban, or suburban.

We have inserted some *fun* images to aid in this journey of exploration. In the late 1940s, important discoveries were made in the Middle East. In Israel, the Dead Sea Scrolls were found hidden in caves near the ruins of an Essene community called Qumran. Around the same time, other ancient manuscripts known as the Nag Hammadi Library that include the so-called Gnostic Gospels were uncovered in Egypt. New revelations are coming to light about life in the ancient Jewish and Christian communities even as scholars continue to study these documents some sixty years later. Just so, we hope that this field guide can bring new insights to those who explore its pages.

The first chapter lays out the challenges for taking this journey today in the midst of being a changing church living within a changing world. The second chapter provides a biblical and theological foundation for taking this journey by exploring a congregation's missional identity. The quest continues by examining the indicators of God's ever-present work among us. These are discussed as seven keys that can assist a congregation as it engages in a journey of transformation. Each chapter also provides references to additional resources that can be pursued as desired. Engage the quest! Enjoy the journey!

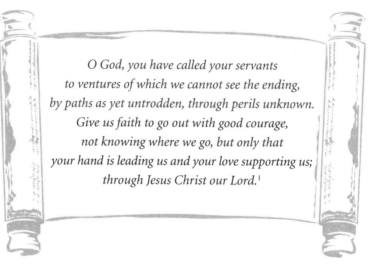

O God, you have called your servants
to ventures of which we cannot see the ending,
by paths as yet untrodden, through perils unknown.
Give us faith to go out with good courage,
not knowing where we go, but only that
your hand is leading us and your love supporting us;
through Jesus Christ our Lord.[1]

1

Does the Church Have a Future?

What Is God Up To?

The speaker was trying to be gracious, but he also wanted to be honest. Addressing a large number of pastors of a midsized mainline denomination, he remarked, "You know, if the 1950s ever come back, your congregations are well prepared to respond."

Unfortunately, this is the case with so many congregations today. Their identity, as well as their approach to ministry, was shaped by another time and place—such as the 1950s period of suburban success for the church. Today, many congregations do not have a clear connection with the contexts in which they now find themselves. The 1950s are not going to come back. At that time, the Christian church still enjoyed a privileged position in society. This was symbolized by such things as prayer in public schools, nativity scenes on court house lawns, regular denominational broadcasting on radio, and the emerging world of network television. Such conditions allowed for an approach to ministry by congregations that assumed people were still seeking out the church.

We now find ourselves at some distance from that time in a location often described as "postmodern."[1] The postmodern era has brought with it a resurgence of spirituality. This is occurring, however, alongside of a significant decline of commitment to institutional forms of religion, which is especially true for the emerging generation who often seek less formal expressions of the church. Some segments of mainline Christianity are showing signs of vibrancy in this changed context, but congregations that are involved in this vibrancy are definitely finding themselves to be on a journey that is much like a quest, one requiring them to rethink their identity as they consider new approaches to ministry.

Where Are We?

There is no question that the twenty-first century, mainline Christian church in the United States is in peril. Membership numbers, worship attendance, and a host of other statistics from denominational offices support this claim. It appears that many mainline congregations in the United States seem destined to repeat the fate of their cousins in Europe where church attendance is at an all-time low. A 2005 survey conducted by *Newsweek* magazine reveals that the Christian church is in decline in Europe and the United States. The same article, however, noted differences in church decline in the west, where a Gallup poll found that on average only 15 percent of people in Europe attend weekly worship compared with 44 percent in the United States.

One has only to look at the specific statistics from mainline denominations in the United States to see the shift taking place. According to research conducted by the Gallup organization, mainline denominations peaked by the 1960s, and many mainline congregations have been in serious decline for nearly forty years. Some denominations have diminished by nearly 50 percent. According to Albert Winseman, Gallup's leader for studying faith-based organizations, an ominous sign is that congregational membership is shrinking in proportion to the United States population. "Congregational membership in the United States increased by almost 9% in the decade between 1990 and 2000. But the overall U.S. population increased by a little more than 13% during that same time. Church membership growth is not keeping up with population growth. The church is losing ground."[2]

Membership in the Evangelical Lutheran Church in America (ELCA) declined by 5.7 percent between 1999 and 2005, a loss of nearly 300,000 members. Even more alarming, ELCA congregations confirmed 14 percent fewer youth during that same time frame, substantiating that the median age of ELCA members is now much older than the population in general. Worship trends as reported by the 10,640 ELCA congregations are also a cause for concern: over 76 percent are in decline or merely maintaining attendance.

In Decline	Stable/Maintaining	Growing
46.1%	30.1%	23.8%
(more than 5% loss)	*(less than 5% loss or gain)*	*(more than 5% gain)*

The ELCA's Grand Canyon Synod, comprised of Arizona and southern Nevada, exemplifies the church's failing to effectively reach new people. While the population of these states increased by 23 percent over a six-year period (1999–2005), ELCA congregations in the Grand Canyon Synod experienced an overall membership loss of 3.5 percent. During that same time, worship attendance in ELCA congregations decreased by 1 percent.[3] In an area experiencing the largest population growth nationwide, including the two fastest growing cities in the United States—Phoenix and Las Vegas—the ELCA is undeniably losing ground.

In the early 1990s, church demographer Loren Meade suggested in his groundbreaking study of religion in America, *The Once and Future Church*, that the church as we know it must die in order to be resurrected into a new form through the work of the Holy Spirit.[4] Without making any judgments one way or another about Meade's prognosis for the church, one thing is certain: most mainline congregations will need to rethink their identity and reframe their approach to ministry if they are going to survive, let alone prosper.

Facing New Realities

The consultant was into the first session on Friday evening of what was designed as a weekend retreat for the church council to engage in some strategic planning. This opening presentation was intended to set up the need to engage in strategic planning by describing the various changes taking place in both the congregation and the community it served. The word "change" had probably been used at least twenty times in the first thirty minutes when an elder from the council raised his hand. The consultant acknowledged the hand and the elder commented, "We as the council have discovered that using the word 'change' makes many of our members feel uncomfortable, so we voted recently not to use that word." The consultant thought to himself, "Well, that solves the problem; just vote change out of existence." He proceeded to use the word "development" the rest of the weekend.

It doesn't make much difference what word one uses, the reality is that congregations today find themselves in a very different place now than a few decades ago. There is a joke shared in church circles that quips, "How many Lutherans does it take to change a light bulb?" And the response is always a puzzled, "Change?" This is a humorous illustration indicating a church often reluctant to change. A 2007 survey of ELCA congregations clearly indicates that more than 40 percent of them were *not* ready to try something new.[5] Perhaps this resistance to change is the reason that many congregations are finding it hard to connect with people outside the church. Unfortunately, many are yet to discover that they are in decline as a result of this reluctance.

As noted above, U.S. culture has changed drastically over the past several decades. Congregations must open their eyes to our changing context. The Bible teaches us that the living God through the Spirit is present in the midst of what is currently taking place. God's active presence in congregations and their larger contexts invites congregations to rethink their identity and to reframe their approach to ministry in order to more faithfully participate in God's mission. This is what we are referring to as becoming "missional congregations." We have found church leader and author Reggie McNeal's naming of the following six new realities to be helpful for missional congregations to consider.[6]

New Reality One: The Collapse of the Church Culture

No longer can it be assumed that most members of the community are members of a congregation. Nor can it be assumed that most people in the community have an understanding of the teachings of the church. Surveys indicate that a majority of people are biblically illiterate.[7]

New Reality Two: The Shift from Church Growth to Kingdom Growth

For too long, many congregations have focused on growing by simply adding members who transferred from other congregations and through the bearing of children. They have failed to follow up on one of the most important tasks prescribed by Jesus himself—faithfully bearing witness to the kingdom of God—which normally leads to the growing of new disciples. Congregations are called to be about making disciples in relation to God's kingdom, helping people grow in their faith and equipping them to participate more fully in God's mission in the world.

New Reality Three: A New Reformation—Releasing God's People for Ministry

Congregations have done reasonably well in recruiting and training people to serve the needs of the institutional church. What has suffered is the broader participation of many congregations in God's mission in the world, especially outreach to those of no faith, little faith, or other faiths within a congregation's own local context. Luther's idea of the priesthood of all believers was that all Christians are called in baptism to carry out their vocational ministries in daily life—in *all* arenas of life, including in the workplace, the community, and the home, as well as in the church. All God's baptized are the frontline missionaries for the gospel in their local contexts for the sake of the world.

New Reality Four: The Return to Spiritual Formation

How do we adequately nurture people in the faith and prepare them to live out their lives in the world? A congregation must take seriously its responsibility of cultivating spiritual formation. It must attend carefully and intentionally to the work of helping Christians experience spiritual transformation, so they can live out their faith with courage, confidence, and hope. Congregations are to help the body as a whole, as well as groups of believers and individuals, exercise their spiritual muscles. As such, a congregation serves as a "spiritual fitness center."

New Reality Five: The Shift from Planning to Preparation

Congregations are often so preoccupied with meetings for the sake of planning and discussing policy that people are hungry for experiencing the Spirit's leading and are searching for opportunities to engage in "hands on" ministry. There is some value in considering the Nike slogan of "just do it" in regard to giving people permission to try new things as they actively discern the Spirit's leading in their midst. Congregational structures need to be designed to promote such *permission giving* and cooperation among church leaders and members, resulting in empowerment and support for the ministry of all God's people in the church and in the world.

New Reality Six: The Rise of Apostolic Leadership

Congregations need visionary leaders who are committed to bearing witness to God's kingdom, who are not seeking primarily the building of the kingdom of their own congregations. Such leaders must learn to think *outside the box* and be open to the leading of God's Spirit. The fields today are also "ripe for the harvest" (John 4:35), so bold, Spirit-led, God-fearing leaders are needed to lead the church into a new, exciting future—a quest that becomes a journey of transformation.

Changing Paradigms

It's been said that the seven last words of the church are "we've never done it that way before." The truth is that in order for the church to effectively reach people with the good news of God's love in an ever-changing world, we will need to deeply explore our identity—being missional, while also embracing doing things in new ways and utilizing a changed ministry approach. The premise of this book is that becoming an effective witness to the gospel in today's world—becoming a missional congregation—requires us to revision the way we *are* the church in order to more faithfully *do* church. Consider the following shifts in an understanding of what the church is and does.

FROM:	TO :
Maintenance	Mission
Membership	Discipleship
Pastor-Centered	Lay-Empowered
Chaplaincy (Self)	Hospitality (Others)
Focus On Ourselves	Focus On The World
Settled	Sent

This set of contrasting emphases is in many ways about moving past the functional Christendom model that reinforced the church's privileged status in society. As we think of designing congregations for a new century of mission, we are inclined to return to the example of the early church in the New Testament that made no assumptions about the culture supporting the church or the Christian message. Congregations need to learn how to participate in the mission of God as the doorway to discovering a new identity. The Great Commission of Jesus is at the heart of God's mission: "go into all the world and make disciples."[8] If we took this command of Jesus seriously, we would understand that the front door of every church and indeed of every Christian opens up onto a mission field.

The missional church is not about maintenance or survival as an institution, but rather about participating more fully in God's mission. It is not focused so much on the number of members, but rather on how well people are living out their faith in daily discipleship. Its ministry is not so much centered on the work of the pastor, but rather on empowering the laity (nonclergy) for their ministry in daily life. While a chaplaincy church may view caring for its members as an end in itself, a missional congregation will provide care as a *means to an end*—to help its disciples be healthy and effective in their efforts to reach out to others with the love of God in Christ.

Missional congregations practice the kind of hospitality that welcomes the stranger even while anticipating that welcoming new people to share in ministry may change their faith community. Ministry in these congregations is not designed just to meet the needs of its own members (in-reach), but to help meet the needs of those in the larger community (outreach). Finally, this is not a "settled" church comfortable with the status quo, but rather a "sent" church that sees itself as on the move for the sake of gospel and the sake of the world.

Redefining Roles

As the diagram below illustrates, roles change in the missional congregation as it seeks to participate in God's mission in the world. First, laity become the frontline ministers. Second, church professionals train and support the ministry of all the baptized people of God. Third, we understand that ministry is more than what happens in church. It also includes what takes place through the vocations of today's disciples within their daily lives for the sake of the world.

Post-Christendom Paradigm Shift

Everyone a Minister   Care of members is not end in itself, but "means to end"—nurturing disciples.

Trainers: Staff & Leaders   Staff train and empower missionaries.

Purpose: Mission Outreach   Members are frontline missionaries.

For the Sake of the World—Externally Focused Congregations

Missional congregations need to keep the world in focus as their larger horizon. They need to become externally focused. Flying a small plane provides a helpful example of an externally focused congregation. This is the purpose of the aircraft—to fly! A pilot keeps one eye focused out the window while keeping the other eye on the instruments. The pilot needs to be externally focused while also attending to what the instruments are conveying in order to help ensure a safe flight. So it is with a missional congregation.

In their book, *The Externally Focused Church*, Rick Rusaw and Eric Swanson write about congregations that are making a difference by reaching out to meet the needs of hurting people in their communities. Such congregations live their lives for the sake of the world. They are externally focused. These are their defining characteristics:

- They are inwardly strong but outwardly focused.
- They integrate good deeds and good news into the life of the congregation.
- They value impact and influence in the community more than attendance.
- They seek to be salt, light, and leaven in the community.
- They would be greatly missed by the community if they left.[9]

How many churches today would be missed by anyone outside of their own congregational membership if they ceased to exist? Would the larger community even notice?

Missional Theology

Underlying this is a deeper theological understanding. The word *missional* was introduced to the church's vocabulary in the late 1990s and popularized by pastors, church leaders, and seminary professors who were part of a group known as The Gospel and Our Culture Network.[10] They were seeking to help congregations in the United States better understand how to respond to their rapidly changing contexts.

These persons were fully aware of many of the programs for church health and church effectiveness that were available to congregations for addressing such change, such as Purpose-Driven Church, Alpha, Natural Church Development, and others like them. While recognizing the value of such approaches, they knew that before turning to the question of "What should a congregation *do*?" they needed to explore more deeply the question of the identity of the church and ask, "What should a congregation *be*?" They explored the deeper question of "Why did God create the church?" More specifically they asked, "Why does God create local congregations?"

Based on the clear teaching of Scripture, these questions assume something about God's agency—that God is present and is directly acting in the world. They assume that God's actions through the Spirit can to some extent be discerned in our midst. These basic scriptural commitments require us to focus on the very *identity* of congregations—their nature or essence—as the key to understanding how to help them respond to all the changes taking place in the world around them.[11] The key premise of the missional church is that what a congregation *does* needs to be deeply informed by what a congregation *is*—what God has made and is making it to be.

Case Study: The Importance of Transformation

The following is a composite picture illustrating circumstances experienced in many congregations. This story is based on the accounts of several real congregations that underwent a journey of transformation in order to discover new life and purpose.

Ten years ago Amazing Grace Church built a new four-million-dollar campus, raising all but about one million dollars. This was viewed as a huge success at the time. Worship attendance was averaging 500 each week. There was a vital Sunday school and youth program, and there were 200 children on the church campus every day in the preschool, kindergarten, and day care. The congregation also boasted of an after school program that included a music and arts academy. At one point, the program staff included three pastors, a Director of Education, a Youth Director, a Director of the Kids Academy, and several part-time music staff, including a coordinator for contemporary wor-ship. The church was involved in significant community outreach, and the congregation's annual ministry budget was over three quarters of a million dollars per year.

Following the major building program, conflict developed between the staff and some key lay leaders in the congregation. The pastor decided to resign and went to serve another congregation in a neigh-boring town. Many members of the congregation were surprised and shocked at her sudden departure. Some blamed the church leader-ship for the loss of their beloved pastor. The resulting turmoil saw a loss in membership and financial support.

Several interim pastors were appointed by the bishop over a three-year period, none of them serving more than a year, so there was little or no stability. Membership loss and a decline in giving caused staff and programs to be cut. One of the interim pastors decided that, for one year, there would be no Sunday school, vacation Bible school, or youth program. Over that same period, three worship services were eventually cut to one and attendance plummeted to about two hun-dred each week.

Finally, a new lead pastor was called to serve the congregation and he began to rebuild a team of committed staff and lay leaders, bringing to the congregation a renewed focus on God's mission and discipleship. Some ministries were immediately reinstated and a sec-ond worship service with contemporary-style music was added within six months. Over a period of eighteen months, average attendance climbed to three hundred and fifty per week; over one hundred and twenty new members joined the congregation, including a number of unchurched families; more than fifty baptisms were conducted, many of youth and adults; member giving was above budget estimates; and the congregation completed one of its most ambitious stewardship pledge drives in recent memory by raising about 25 percent more in pledges than the previous year. In addition, the congregation con-ducted a successful debt-reduction campaign, surpassing its goal of over a half-million dollars with the aim of cutting mortgage payments *in half and repurposing an annual savings of over $60,000 toward expanding mission and ministry.*

Most important of all, the climate was transformed. Hopefulness has replaced discouragement and despair. For the people of Amazing Grace Church, there is now a renewed sense of identity and purpose, a new spirit of unity, new energy for ministry, and a spirit of excitement about the future. The congregation is effectively reaching out to unchurched people in their community, and membership and worship attendance are up significantly. Finally, the leadership is moving forward with boldness to achieve the missional objectives of their five-year strategic plan.

How did this happen? What insights might be gleaned from this story of transformation? We invite you to join us through the pages of this field guide to engage in a quest that will become your journey of discovery as we consider together what a missional church looks like and how congregations might participate more fully in God's mission in the world. We're glad to have you on this quest, but we warn you to proceed with caution. You and your congregation could be changed forever.

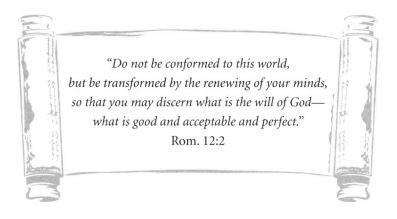

"Do not be conformed to this world,
but be transformed by the renewing of your minds,
so that you may discern what is the will of God—
what is good and acceptable and perfect."
Rom. 12:2

Discovery Questions

1. What are the signs that the mainline church in the United States may be in a state of crisis?

2. How do you view the present health of your own congregation? What indications of vitality do you see? What are the danger signs that it may be in trouble?

3. It is said that change is the only constant. In what ways might it be important for your congregation to change in order to be more responsive to the larger community it seeks to serve? How prepared is your congregation to handle any necessary change?

4. How is the word *missional* being used today? What possibilities does the meaning and use of this word offer your congregation in thinking about its own ministry?

Additional Resources for the Journey

Best, Steven and Douglas Kellner. *The Postmodern Turn.* New York: Guilford, 1997.

Bosch, David. *Transforming Mission: Paradigm Shifts in Theology of Mission.* Maryknoll, N.Y.: Orbis, 2006.

Killen, Patricia and Mark Silk. *Religion and Public Life in the Pacific Northwest: The None Zone.* Lanham, Md.: AltaMira, 2004.

McNeal, Reggie. *The Present Future: Six Tough Questions for the Church.* San Francisco: Jossey-Bass, 2003.

Rusaw, Rick and Eric Swanson. *The Externally Focused Church.* Loveland, Colo.: Group, 2004.

Winseman, Albert. *Growing an Engaged Church: How to Stop Doing Church and Start Being the Church Again.* New York: Gallup, 2007.

2

A Missional Identity: God's Vision for Congregations

Conversation among council members of Amazing Grace Church at the month's regular meeting focused on the rather sharp decline in membership and worship attendance that the council had been monitoring for the past three years. However, a gradual decline had actually been occurring for the past two decades due to the inability of the congregation to respond to new and changing populations in its community. At previous meetings the council had discussed some of these factors and had noted: (a) the aging demographic of much of the Anglo population; (b) the young Anglo families buying starter homes; (c) the transient population in the numerous apartment buildings constructed in the past two decades; and (d) an increase in the number of upwardly mobile Hispanic residents.

John suggested that it was time to quit analyzing the problem and to search for solutions. He mentioned that a friend of his in a Baptist congregation found the Alpha program to be successful in attracting new members. Mary Ann said that she was aware that the ELCA's Evangelical Outreach and Congregational Ministry unit was using something called Natural Church Development to help vitalize congregations.

At this point in the conversation, Steve raised a different kind of question and asked, "Is becoming vital in ministry really about finding the right program or employing the right strategy? I wonder if there isn't something more basic about being the church of Jesus Christ in the world that needs to be considered." Pastor Mark commented that this was an important issue and volunteered to lead a Bible study on it at the next council meeting.

Congregations like Amazing Grace often struggle with how to address a changing context that seems to be contributing to membership decline. Occasionally, they even struggle with a deeper question of why they actually exist as a congregation. This is the issue Steve was raising for the council. This can be a healthy struggle, one that has to do with a congregation's *identity*. One of the most important things a congregation can do is to ask the right questions. Such questions include: "Why does God, through the work of the Spirit, bring congregations into existence?" And even more importantly, "Why did God bring our particular congregation into existence?"

The Church Has a Dual Nature

The key to understanding a congregation's identity is to understand its very nature, or essence. This is also where we must begin to gain perspective for understanding what has become known as the *missional church*. Scripture teaches us that it is God the Spirit who creates the church (Acts 2:1-4). In doing so, the Spirit gives to the church a holy nature in the midst of its humanness (2 Cor. 5:17, Eph. 4:23-24). This means that a congregation has two natures. This is illustrated below.

Holy   Divine   Theological   *(as seen from above)*

Church

Human   Historical   Sociological   *(as seen from below)*

It is the Spirit who creates a congregation as a different kind of community, one that is simultaneously holy and human. It is this same Spirit who leads a congregation into ministry in the world as it seeks to live into the power of its new nature as it lives within the limits of its humanness. The church is the only organization of its kind in the world.

The Human Side of a Congregation's Identity

A congregation's humanness makes its life and ministry quite concrete. Every congregation comes into existence within a particular geographic location, in a particular cultural context, speaking a particular language, and in association with a particular faith perspective within the Christian tradition. These human aspects of a congregation's existence have profound implications for Amazing Grace.

Amazing Grace Church is a fifty-year-old, first-ring suburban Lutheran congregation that speaks English. It is located in a larger community of 1960s starter homes where the Anglo population is now aging and where some Spanish-speaking residents are moving in. The sanctuary was built in the early 1960s with an architectural design of that period and a large two-story educational wing was completed in the early 1970s. However, this space is now underutilized because there are far fewer children and youth in the congregation than there were during the peak of the baby boom years.

These very concrete aspects of a congregation—location, faith tradition, language, and cultural context—all contribute to its identity. They represent aspects of the human side of the dual nature of a congregation. Other aspects of the human side can also be noted, such as the building that houses a congregation and its architectural style, the size of membership and worship attendance, the style of worship and number of services offered, the type of organizational structure that is utilized, and so on. All such human dimensions contribute to shaping a congregation's identity.

These human aspects of a congregation's life represent both its opportunities and its challenges. How can a congregation best utilize the human side of its identity to enhance its ministry? To do this, a congregation must understand the other side of its nature, that it is also holy.

The Holy Side of a Congregation's Identity

It is God the Spirit that brings congregations into existence as communities of God's people in the world. This work of God deeply informs the identity of a congregation and helps to clarify why it exists. Additionally, this helps a congregation gain perspective and to appropriate the power of God that is available from the new nature that it has been given. Congregations are called by God to live their lives by a different set of values—redeemed values—that express the spiritual fruit and Christian practices of their new nature (Gal. 5:22-23; Rom. 12:9-13).

Scripture makes God's intent clear regarding why congregations are created by the Spirit. There are three essential truths that stand out, each of which needs to deeply inform the identity of congregations.

God is a creating God who has a plan for the world. God makes this plan known in Scripture, beginning with the creation account in the book of Genesis and ending with the new heaven and new earth in the book of Revelation. We are not left to ponder the intent of God. God created the world and has a plan for all of life within that world. God's intent is that all of life flourish.

God is a redeeming God who seeks to bring all of life into reconciled relationship. The reality of sin deeply disrupted God's intent for creation. God's solution was to bring about reconciliation within God's creation. It was a radical solution, one that required God's own Son to be born of human flesh. Jesus did this so that he could take on our sin and overcome the power of evil in the world through his death and resurrection.

God works out this reconciliation in the world through people. Throughout the ages, God has always had a people to bear witness to the power and presence of this reconciling God in their midst. The makeup of this people changed over time, but the always present constant was a people who named the name of the living and true God, who served as ambassadors for making God's reconciliation available and known to all. These divine aspects of a congregation's existence have profound implications for Amazing Grace.

Amazing Grace congregation is a unique community created by the Spirit that is called, formed, and sent by God to bear witness to the good news of Jesus Christ within its first-ring suburban location to all—young and old, Anglo and Hispanic, long-term residents and those who are more transient. This congregation is to live as a reconciled community of believers who enact the saving grace of God in their relationships with one another and with those they encounter within their larger community. And they are to continually discern the Spirit's leading in their congregational life and within their larger community as they seek to participate in God's mission in the world within their particular location.

Understanding What It Means to Be a Missional Congregation

The primary way the people of God exist in the world today is in the form of congregations. Congregations are at the center of God's plan and purpose. They bear witness through the Spirit to the reconciling power of God through Christ in their midst by living as a reconciled community. They also bear witness through the Spirit of this reconciling power of God to the larger community in which they minister. Congregations are unique in that they represent God in the world, being formed by the Spirit as particular communities that live in dynamic relationship within their larger communities. This perspective needs to stand at the core of a congregation's identity.

As noted earlier, the *purpose* of a congregation—what it *does*—can only be clearly understood by exploring its *identity* (or its nature or essence)—what a congregation *is*.

Amazing Grace needs to draw deeply on an understanding of why God through the Spirit brought them into existence in their first-ring suburban community in order to understand how to respond to the changes that are now taking place within this context.

So, how does a congregation live out its identity of being both holy and human in carrying out its ministry? In what ways does missional theology inform how congregations are to live in the world? These are important questions to be considered, and they are taken up in the following sections, which deal with the Triune God and the leading of the Spirit.

Missional Theology and the Triune God

The most important theological perspective that shapes missional theology starts with understanding the Triune God. The concept of God as being Trinity is basic to the Christian faith. Understanding God's existence as involving three persons is clearly evident in Scripture, although the formal theological development of this understanding came later through extensive debates, during the first several centuries of the Christian church.

The details of these debates go beyond what is required here, but the key point to be noted is that the early church fully comprehended the crucial importance of understanding God as a Triune God. They settled on the basic view that is now accepted as being part of the historic Christian faith—God is three in one and one in three. Each of these insights deeply informs an understanding of missional theology. The first has to do with understanding the Trinity as being a community within itself, often called the social Trinity. The second has to do with understanding the Trinity as being fully engaged with all the world, through both creation and redemption, often called a sending Trinity.

The Trinity as a Relational Community

Pastor Mark, as promised, was in the midst of leading the Bible study on the nature of the church at the following month's council meeting.

He was exploring several biblical images that spoke of the church as a community of persons in deep relationship with one another— body of Christ, communion of saints, and people of God. Mary Ann, in reflecting on this, raised the question, "Is there any way in which the church's being a relational community is connected with God being a Triune God?" Pastor Mark commented, "Great question," and proceeded to make that connection.

The Triune God is, in fact, a relational community made up of three persons. In theological terms, this is often referred to as the "social Trinity." Scripture makes it clear that the relationships within God—Father, Son, and Spirit—are based on a shared equality. This means that these relationships are nonhierarchical. The community within the Godhead provides a key perspective for understanding the work of God in the world. The church, brought into existence through the redemptive work of Christ, is created by the Spirit as a community of persons who are in relationship with one another because they have become reconciled in Christ.

Implications for Congregations

All human beings are created in the image of God and are created for community. It is part of their very nature to be in relationship with other humans. It is the presence of God through Christ in the world that makes possible the creation of congregations as communities where persons are able to live in reconciled relationship with one another.

Congregations are unique communities within the world. The relationships people express and experience with one another are to be based on equality and mutuality. Power is to be exercised *with* others rather than *over* others, and is grounded in our being servants to one another (Matt. 20:26-27).

The Trinity as a Sending God

As Pastor Mark continued his Bible study with the council, he began working with the incarnation as a demonstration of God's radical love for all the world, a love that led to sending God's only Son to be born of human flesh. John wondered out loud with the group, "If God's love led God to send Jesus into the world, is there any way in which God's love for the world also leads to God sending us as the church into the world?" Again, Pastor Mark commented, "Great question," and proceeded to speak about God sending both the Son and the church.

Understanding the Triune God as a sending God is foundational for understanding how the church is called and sent to participate in God's mission in the world. This perspective understands that the Triune God is intimately involved with the created world. The Triune God is a God that both creates and redeems. These works of God are clearly laid out in Scripture. They involve all three persons of the Godhead.

- The Father planned for and introduced both creation and redemption.
- The Son carried out both creation and redemption.
- The Spirit continues to work within creation to bring redemption to bear on all of life.

This understanding of the Triune God stresses the work of the three persons of God in light of God's one nature. In theological terms, this is usually referred to as the "sending Trinity." Here, attention is placed on the sending work of God. God sent the Son into the world to accomplish redemption, and the Father and the Son continue to send the Spirit into the world to create the church and lead it into participation in God's mission.

Implications for Congregations

Because congregations are called, formed, and sent by the Spirit of God, congregations are missionary by nature. They exist to participate in God's mission in the world by engaging the local context in which they live.

Congregations are responsible to seek to participate in God's mission by engaging in careful discernment of the Spirit's leading in their midst and in the larger community in which they exist.

The Ministry of the Spirit

God's intent of reconciliation is directly towards the world. This ties the work of God in redemption directly to the work of God in creation. There are three aspects to the ministry of the Spirit of God in relation to congregations—sanctified living, ministry in the world, and being used to unmask the principalities and powers. This is what congregations look like when they are living out of an understanding of being a missional church.

The Spirit's Ministry of Sanctified Living

It is the Spirit of God who leads congregations into sanctified living. They are to live consistent with their new nature, which has been given by the Spirit, so that they might participate more fully in God's mission in the world. Paul makes it clear in Romans 8 that a new way of life is to be enjoyed by those who are in Christ—a new life that is led by the Spirit. It is the "Spirit of life" who has set us free from "the law of sin and death" (v. 2). We are no longer subject to the demands of the flesh since these were put to death through Christ's death. This now allows the church to "walk not according to the flesh but according to the Spirit" (v. 4). In light of this new reality of the Spirit's indwelling, the church is invited to "put to death the deeds of the body" (v. 13). It is by the grace given through the Spirit's presence that the church is empowered to do this.

We find in Galatians that *living by the Spirit* and *being guided by the Spirit* are to be the marks of the church (Gal. 5:25). In light of the new nature we have been given, we are now free to experience and express the fruits of the Spirit: love, joy, peace, patience, kindness, generosity, faithfulness, gentleness, and self-control (v. 22-23). Clearly the communities of reconciled diversity that the Spirit creates now have not only the *responsibility* but also the *power* to live by a different set of values in the world. It is this communal lifestyle that displays contrasting values to those of the world, where this lifestyle serves as the basis for the church having an effective witness in the world.

Implication for Congregations
The Spirit of God is actively present in the lives of congregations, help-ing to form them to live out the fruits the Spirit brings and the Christian practices they are responsible to exercise through the Spirit's power.

The Spirit's Ministry of Leading Congregations into the World

The Spirit is the agency of God who brings God's gifts into the life and ministry of the church. This is based on the gifts Christ gives to the church (Eph. 4:7-8), and manifests itself in each participant in the church being the recipient of the Spirit's gifts. "To each is given the manifestation of the Spirit for the common good" (1 Cor. 12:7). This means that members need to discover their gifts and find their place in the body of Christ. Paul makes a major point of trying to help the Corinthian church understand that each person and each gift is impor-tant, and that believers are, in fact, interdependent with one another.

These gifts of the Spirit are not primarily for the recipients' ben-efit. Rather they are given both for the *sake of the body* and for the *sake of the world*. As the gifts are exercised in a congregation, grace flows through the ministry that takes place so that people become "members one of another" (Rom. 12:5), which results in promoting "the body's growth in building itself up in love" (Eph. 4:16). As these gifts are exercised by God's people, ministry also becomes manifest in the world (Rom. 12:14-21). The world is always the larger horizon of God's intent and the Spirit's ministry.

Implication for Congregations
Congregations are to be living demonstrations to the watching world within their local contexts that God is the living and true God, and that God's redemptive and reconciling love is freely and graciously available to all.

The Spirit's Ministry of Unmasking the Principalities and Powers

The church encounters the reality of sin and the brokenness of the world as the Spirit leads the church into the world to participate in

God's mission. We find that believers, along with creation itself, "groan inwardly" as all await release from the bondage of sin (Rom. 8:18-24). But while the church lives in this in-between time, it also encounters the forces of evil that the Bible refers to as the "principalities and powers" (also translated as "rulers and authorities") (Eph. 6:12). These powers seek to thwart the ministry of the Spirit. But God in Christ defeated these principalities and powers and showed them to be without ultimate authority (Col. 2:15). Now the Spirit is leading the church into the world to demonstrate this reality by unmasking the powers through the Spirit's ministry through the church (Eph. 3:10).

This ministry of unmasking the powers does not come through triumphalism, but rather follows the way of the cross in a lifestyle of suffering service (Mark 10:45; Rom. 8:14-21). This unmasking also does not go uncontested. Yet, we are secure in the love of Christ because God is for us. There is nothing that can separate us from God, whether "hardship, or distress, or persecution, or famine, or nakedness, or peril, or sword" (Rom. 8:35). This promise clearly indicates that the church living out a lifestyle of suffering service under the Spirit's leading will not be exempt from pain and struggle. So the church joyfully enters into ministry in the world to engage in reconciling diversity, extending mercy, and exercising justice, all the while knowing that it will often be misunderstood and mistreated, but also knowing that the grace of Christ is sufficient (2 Cor. 12:9).

Implication for Congregations

Congregations must understand that there is a larger spiritual reality that exists all around them, and that how they live their lives and carry out their ministries is a part of this larger reality. They participate in this larger work of God's Spirit by enacting reconciliation through a lifestyle of suffering service within their life and through their ministry to the powers embedded within their local context.

Congregations are central to God's work in the world. They have a dual nature of being both holy and human, which makes them unique.

They are called, formed, and sent to participate in God's mission of reconciliation within their local contexts. They do this by enacting the reconciliation that God makes available through Christ both within their life as a congregation and in relation to the larger community they seek to serve. The challenge that is always before them is how to respond to changing local contexts.

Discovery Questions

1. How would you summarize what is meant by the "missional identity" of a congregation? How does this compare with the present identity of your congregation?

2. What does it mean that the church is simultaneously "holy" and "human"? What are the key indicators you would give to describe how your congregation is presently both "holy" and "human"?

3. How does understanding the Trinity help inform the identity of a missional congregation? The social Trinity? The sending Trinity?

4. What does the ministry of the Spirit look like in a missional congregation? What evidence might you cite of the Spirit's leading your congregation in these ways?

Additional Resources for the Journey

Bliese, Richard H. and Craig Van Gelder. *The Evangelizing Church: A Lutheran Contribution.* Minneapolis: Augsburg Fortress, 2005.

Guder, Darrell L. ed. *Missional Church: A Vision for the Sending of the Church in North America.* Grand Rapids, Mich.: Eerdmans, 1988.

Van Gelder, Craig. *The Essence of the Church: A Community Created by the Spirit.* Grand Rapids, Mich.: Baker, 2000.

Van Gelder, Craig. *The Ministry of the Missional Church: A Community Led by the Spirit.* Grand Rapids, Mich.: Baker, 2007.

Van Gelder, Craig, ed., *The Missional Church in Context: Helping Congregations Develop Contextual Ministry.* Grand Rapids, Mich.: Eerdmans, 2007.

Develop a Vision for God's Mission

Upon his arrival, the new pastor of Amazing Grace Church led the congregation through a visioning process that included a series of cottage meetings in homes. Over two months, he met with over 300 members to learn their concerns, hopes, and dreams for the congregation. Now a year later, he decided to repeat the process to "test the waters" and see how the climate in the congregation may have changed.

Members gathered again in small groups during the six weeks of Lent. They were asked to attend at least one meeting with the pastor and a key lay leader in order to share their impressions of what had changed and give their commentary on the direction the congregation seemed to be headed. The comments were overwhelmingly positive:

"I can't believe how much difference a year can make. Instead of feeling discouraged like I did twelve months ago, I am encouraged, hopeful, and excited about what I see happening."

"We are no longer a fractured church, but instead there is a new sense of unity among us."

"We seem to be united around a shared common vision for ministry."

 This is the first transformational key.
Congregations that have a clear vision for ministry are more likely to move forward together than those who seem to lack a common purpose.

Understanding God's Mission and How We Participate in It

Having a shared vision based on a missional identity is crucial for any church that wishes to experience faithful and effective ministry. This helps a congregation develop vitality, and usually leads to growth. According to a study completed by the Department for Research and Evaluation of the Evangelical Lutheran Church in America (ELCA), two common characteristics are exhibited by vital and growing congregations: first, they were clear about their purpose and vision for ministry; and second, these vibrant congregations showed an openness to change in order to be faithful to carrying out God's mission.[1] These congregations ask two important questions: "*What is God's purpose for our ministry?*" and "*What do we need to do to be effective for God's work in this place?*" Congregations who are seeking to answer these questions need to explore three different, but interrelated, aspects pertinent to ministry: missional identity, common purpose, and shared vision.

Congregations are served by cultivating a *missional identity*. As discussed in chapter two, the church has a dual nature of being both holy and human. This means that congregations are created by the Spirit and are called to participate in God's mission in the world. Cultivating a missional identity helps a congregation understand God's agency at work in its midst, and also helps it to maintain perspective when attempting to make decisions about all the concrete realities of ministry life, such as programs, staffing, budgets, and buildings. Developing a missional identity means that congregations deeply understand that they are marked with the cross of Christ forever. It answers the important question, "Why do we exist?" This is about understanding our *being*.

Congregations are served by clarifying a *common purpose*, one that is grounded in their missional identity. The question that is answered here is, "What is God calling us to do?" In exploring this question, a congregation seeks to understand what it is called to *do* in light of what it was created to *be*. A congregation does not have its own mission;

rather it is created, gathered, and sent to participate in God's mission. Clarifying a common purpose helps a congregation focus on how to live its life for God's purposes. This includes caring for all of creation, being an agent of healing and reconciliation in a broken world, and sharing the love of God made known in Jesus Christ with *everyone*, *everywhere*. Congregations are to bear witness to the redemptive reign of God in the world by being a community that enacts in its life and ministry God's grace, mercy, forgiveness, love, justice, and peace in *everything*. How each congregation will participate in God's mission will depend on their own local context. But one thing is certain: God wants to bless the world through the church.

Congregations are further served by developing a *shared vision*. Martin Luther King Jr. looked out at the U.S. context of his day and articulated more clearly than anyone before or since the dream (vision) he had for racial equality in America. This vision inspired a whole generation and changed the nation forever. The same God who inspired King's dream invites congregations to explore deeply the issues embedded in the larger communities they seek to serve, and then to articulate a vision for carrying out a common purpose in their particular context.

The question that needs to be answered here is, "What will it look like if we live out our common purpose in this particular context?" Such a vision is always tailored to a specific context, but it always bears in mind God's vision for the church. God dreams of a church that does not exist primarily to serve its own members, but is committed to transforming lives and being the body of Christ for the sake of the world. God dreams of a church that is focused on making disciples and empowering people to live out their faith in their daily lives.

God's Mission—For the Sake of the World

A major challenge facing congregations in the United States has to do with the horizon they use for framing their life and ministry. When they first come into existence, most congregations are very outreach oriented and seek to actively engage their larger community.

They have the world in view as their primary horizon. Congregations that have matured, however, tend to develop complex ministries focused increasingly on the needs of their own members. Their horizon begins to turn inward toward meeting their own needs.

"The reason God made the church was to call forth a community of allies," according to Dave Daubert, Director of Congregational Renewal for the ELCA. He goes on to say, "God is looking for allies in mission and each of us and each of our congregations has a role to play as God's dream unfolds. That role is our purpose. Mission is God's work to bless and save the world. Our purpose is our part in God's work."[2] Transforming a congregation's ministry means connecting the church with what God is up to in the world.

There is a story about a lighthouse that was built on a cliff above a treacherous stretch of coastline. Many ships, crashing upon the rocks, had met a tragic end and many lives had been lost at sea. So it was decided to form a lighthouse society whose purpose was to tend the light in order to warn sailors of the pending danger and thus save lives. After a while, however, those who were members of the society became distracted with other tasks. Some formed a social club so that members could enjoy one another's company. Others were involved in fund-raising in order to help finance these social gatherings. And so it went, until one day someone forgot to check the fire in the lighthouse and the light went out. Because of the darkness on the coastline that night, several ships were lost at sea. The original purpose of the lighthouse had been displaced.

This parable addresses the identity, purpose, and vision of the church. God's people need to be constantly reminded that above all God created the church through the Spirit for God's purposes in the world. They also need to be reminded that God has called and sent this church into the world to bear witness to God's reign and to the reconciliation of all of life that was accomplished through Christ. And they need to be reminded that they are called to participate in making this redemption available to *everyone, everywhere,* while leading a life that demonstrates that this redemption is about all of life, about *everything.*

If mission is what God is up to, congregations need to ask, "What are we doing to participate more fully in God's mission in our community and in the larger world?" At the same time, congregations will find it helpful to engage in an assessment of their current ministries by asking, "What are we doing that may be hindering our participation in God's mission within our larger community?" It is helpful to have every ministry of a congregation review its work in light of these questions. Congregational ministry team leaders must be willing to see God's mission with new eyes and then take up the challenge of being a new church for a new day.

Participating in God's Mission—A Common Purpose

We encourage the pastoral and lay leaders of congregations to lead their members in a quest of discovery to clarify God's purpose for their ministry. It can be helpful to develop a *purpose statement* that reminds the congregation of what they are called to *do*. We suggest that congregational leaders take a different approach from some of the long, drawn-out purpose statements that were popular in the last decade or so. Most of these include a laundry list of everything a congregation does from worship to learning and service. A purpose statement is most helpful when it is stated succinctly so that people can easily remember it and regularly refer to it. A purpose statement should hone in on what the congregation is about. It should answer the question, "What is God calling us to do?" Consider the examples of an earlier purpose statement at Amazing Grace and its current one.

Old Purpose Statement: *"God's people at Amazing Grace gather to worship and learn and are nurtured in faith so that they can better serve others and reach more people in our community who will become members of our congregation."*

New Purpose Statement: *"Healing hurts, rebuilding dreams, transforming lives."*

The difference between the two is profound. The first statement is largely inwardly focused, and the implied purpose is increasing congregational membership. The statement is also too long to be easily recalled even if printed on a worship bulletin or included in the parish newsletter on a regular basis. The second statement was born of a time of deep discernment about God's plan and purpose for Amazing Grace's ministry following a painful and challenging incident. It became clear during this time of discernment that God wanted to use this tragedy to help Amazing Grace members bring help and healing to others in the community. This statement reflects their renewed sense of identity and purpose. It is focused outward. It is short. And it is easy to remember.

Participating in God's Mission—A Shared Vision

A congregation's vision for its ministry needs to be developed in light of its purpose statement. As noted, developing a vision answers the question, "What will it look like if we live out our common purpose in this particular context?" This requires that a congregation carefully and deeply study the larger community constituting its ministry context.

Congregations need to systematically study their particular contexts to evaluate current trends. City or county planning departments, human service agencies, other local churches, and United States Census information (available online) provide helpful resources. Gathering such information is very beneficial in gaining some perspective on the issues and needs of particular communities. After assembling such information and using it to generate a picture of the community, another step needs to be taken to understand God's mission within this context. This information needs to be read through a biblical and theological lens to discern the work of God taking place in this context.

It is important to bear in mind that changes taking place in congregational contexts always bring with them new opportunities for ministry, as well as challenges that must be addressed. Changing contexts require congregations to regularly ask key questions in relation to the larger communities they seek to serve. The first, "What is God up to?" has to do with the process of continuous discernment. The second, "What does God want to do?" has to do with the parallel process of continuous planning.

What Is God Up To?—The Issue of Discernment

The world belongs to God. It is God's creation. The church must seek to discern what the Spirit of God is doing in relation to the dynamic changes that are taking place within a particular context. These activities of the Spirit often present fresh opportunities for ministry to congregations. It is necessary to note that God is at work in the world beyond the church. Discerning this work of God is foundational for effective ministry because the church is called and sent to participate in God's mission in the world. The responsibility of the church is to discern where and how this mission is unfolding.

What Does God Want To Do?—The Issue of Planning

God's mission includes God's desire to bring all of life into reconciled relationship. The church must seek to understand how this intent of God, as expressed in the gospel, can be worked out within its particular context. How can the church contribute to the ministry of reconciliation within the larger community it seeks to serve? This requires careful planning, and focuses on how the work of the Spirit is related to the redemptive activity of God in the world. For a church to be a steward of the good news of the gospel, it must engage in focused missional planning and consider how to participate in what God wants to do in their context. In the diagram are key elements that need to be considered as a congregation plans its missional strategy.

Developing a Shared Vision for Ministry—A Process

A congregation needs to develop a shared vision for understanding how to live out its common purpose in its particular context. To accomplish this, it can be helpful for a congregation to engage in an intentional visioning process, taking care to include as many congregational members as possible. Following is one account of how this visioning process began in one congregation that accepted God's invitation to embark on a journey of discovery and transformation.

An Invitation to Envision the Future

Upon his arrival the new senior pastor of Amazing Grace Church invited the congregation and its leadership to enter into a visioning process that would help them ascertain what kind of future God had planned for them. Because the congregation had experienced a time of crisis and decline, there was need for both healing and a new sense of purpose and direction. The pastor asked the church council to help select a team of eight people who would guide the process. He requested that these people: 1) know the congregation well, 2) be respected members of the congregation, 3) be diverse in age, gender, ethnic background, and life experience, 4) be spiritually mature, regular at worship, and grounded in God's word, and 5) be visionaries able to think outside the box.

Cottage Meetings

The pastor worked with these eight individuals, known as the vision team, to develop and implement a visioning experience that would involve the entire congregation (see appendix A). To begin the visioning process, a series of twenty cottage meetings was planned for a two-month period. Most of these meetings were held in homes with a member serving as host or hostess. People signed up to attend the cottage meeting of their choice. The role of the host or hostess was to call to remind members of the meeting, welcome them as they arrived, and provide refreshments. One cottage meeting was even held for a group of high school youth.

An Opportunity for Conversation

The pastor and a member of the vision team served as facilitators for the gathering. The team member welcomed everyone, thanked the host or hostess for the hospitality, and outlined the purpose of the meeting. The pastor continued with an opening prayer and short Bible study on the Great Commission (Matt. 28:16-20). Then a survey (see below) was passed out to everyone. After all had completed it, the pastor led a conversation about it, inviting each to answer the first two questions, then opening it up for discussion on the remaining ones. It turned out that it was especially important for people to share on question number two. It was here that feelings about past hurt as well as a sense of hopefulness were expressed openly. A member of the vision team took notes, and at the end of the evening all surveys were collected. The pastor concluded the evening in prayer and expressed appreciation to the group for its willingness to begin dreaming about a new future together.

Vision for Ministry Survey:
"Sharing Our Hopes and Dreams"

1. *How long have you been a member or associated with Amazing Grace Church?*

2. *What three words describe Amazing Grace Church?*

3. *What are some of the strengths of Amazing Grace Church? What do you especially appreciate about our congregation? List at least three things.*

4. *What are your hopes and dreams for the congregation's ministry? What would you like to see happen in the next one to five years?*

5. *What are the primary changes or challenges in our larger community that you feel God is leading us to respond to or address?*

6. *If you could dream big, what could we accomplish in our ministry together in seeking to serve our larger community?*

7. *What are the assets and resources that are available within this congregation for making this dream a reality?*

Developing a Missional Plan

The vision team interviewed members of the staff and key lay leaders in the congregation to assess the congregation's readiness to move forward. The input gathered from the interviews and cottage meetings was sifted through to find common themes, ideas, and strategies. Then the vision team went to work to develop a missional plan that addressed matters of congregational identity, common purpose, and a shared vision. They prepared a document that was first reviewed by the church council, and after being fine-tuned was presented to the congregation at their annual meeting in the spring. During the process, the congregation was kept informed through newsletter articles, temple talks, and an open forum prior to the annual meeting. At the annual meeting a Vision for Ministry strategic planning document was unanimously approved and it became a template for guiding the congregation's ministry over the next five years (see pages 139–142).

King Solomon, son of King David, wrote, "Where there is no vision, the people perish" (Prov. 29:18 KJV). Healthy and vital congregations have a clear sense of purpose and a shared vision for ministry. In contrast, struggling congregations are focused on little more than their own survival. The wise king adds, "Always continue in fear of the Lord. Surely there is a future, and your hope will not be cut off" (Prov. 23:17b-18). It is important for the leaders of a congregation to believe that their congregation is being called to be a part of God's missional future, and that they are inviting people to explore, through prayer, Scripture, and a mutual conversation of discernment, what God's purpose and vision are for their ministry. We invite you to take on the quest and to engage the exciting process of mutual discernment of what God is calling you to *be* and to *do* in your particular ministry setting. Then together, as you clarify your missional identity, your common purpose, and your shared vision, you can decide how to faithfully take the journey of more faithfully participating in God's mission as you live into a new future.

Discovery Questions

1. Why is it important for a congregation to develop a missional identity? How would a missional identity inform your congregation's life and ministry?

2. What is meant when we speak of God's mission, and how does this inform how a congregation develops a common purpose for its ministry?

3. What is your congregation's current purpose statement? How might this be improved so that both leaders and members of your congregation can readily and easily articulate and support it?

4. Given the particulars of the larger community your congregation is seeking to serve, what would you discern to be God's vision and plan for your congregation?

5. In what ways can having a vision for ministry help to unify a congregation as well as better focus the use of its resources?

Resources for the Journey

Ammerman, Nancy T., et al. *Studying Congregations: A New Handbook*. Nashville: Abingdon, 1998.

Daubert, Dave. *Living Lutheran: Renewing Your Congregation*. Minneapolis: Augsburg Fortress, 2007.

Kallestad, Walt. *Turn Your Church Inside Out: Building a Community for Others*. Minneapolis: Augsburg Fortress, 2001.

McClaren, Brian. *Church on the Other Side: Exploring the Radical Future of the Local Congregation*. Grand Rapids, Mich.: Zondervan, 2005.

Nessan, Craig. *Beyond Maintenance to Mission: A Theology of the Congregation*. Minneapolis: Augsburg Fortress, 1999.

Focus on God's Mission and Discipleship

The pastor and chair of the Outreach Ministry Team were meeting with a couple who were longtime members of the church. The couple had expressed some displeasure about some of the changes happening in the congregation since the arrival of the new pastor.

"We are trying some new things in order to reach the many people in our community who have no church home," explained Jim, the outreach team chair.

"Why should we care about all those people out there?" questioned the husband of the couple. "Our church should pay more attention to those of us who have been around for the past forty years!"

Jim, normally soft spoken and mild mannered, nearly jumped across the table, startling the couple. "It is those people out there who we are called to share the good news with! If we don't care about them, we might as well close our doors. Don't you remember that Jesus told us we were to go into all the world and make disciples?!"

Who is right? Should the church focus all its energy and resources on reaching new people for Christ? In doing so, are we ignoring the needs and concerns of longtime members? Or is there some kind of balance that each congregation should strive for?

This is the second transformational key.
*Congregations that focus on becoming a discipling commu-
nity as they deeply engage their context are more likely to
develop a healthy life that moves beyond institutional survival or just serving the needs of its members.*

A Biblical Understanding of Transformation

It is important to understand spiritual transformation as being the
basis for both our practice of discipleship and our becoming a discipling community. This is the transformational ministry of the Spirit
in the life of a congregation. The biblical framework for understanding spiritual transformation is laid out by the apostle Paul.

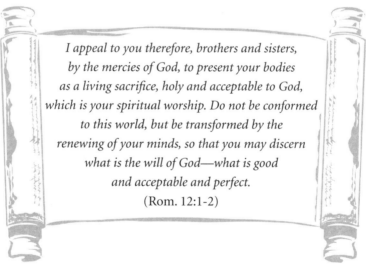

*I appeal to you therefore, brothers and sisters,
by the mercies of God, to present your bodies
as a living sacrifice, holy and acceptable to God,
which is your spiritual worship. Do not be conformed
to this world, but be transformed by the
renewing of your minds, so that you may discern
what is the will of God—what is good
and acceptable and perfect.*
(Rom. 12:1-2)

Paul establishes the important relationship between a congregation's *being* (understanding and accepting what God has done and
what the Spirit is doing) and a congregation's *doing* (our responsibilities to act on this reality in carrying out the ministry of reconciliation
that has been given to us).

Paul addresses the Roman congregation in terms of how they should
live in light of the mercies of God that have been given to Christian

believers—the grace of God extended in salvation. The grammatical structure of this chapter is important to note. In verses 1–2, Paul uses a series of plural nouns and pronouns (your bodies, your, you) in relation to a variety of singular objects (one living sacrifice, one worship, one mind, one will of God). His point is that our corporate life is to come to expression as singular outcomes. Congregations are to live their lives as a corporate community.

Paul is inviting the Roman congregation to understand its unity in the midst of its diversity. By becoming a corporate living sacrifice, they communally express true spiritual worship (or service). Paul is asserting that this relationally reconciled community should then be able to come to a common mind in *discerning* the will of God. This discerning process is to be an active engagement where the participants struggle through their differences to come to a common agreement.

The council at Amazing Grace is in the midst of such a discernment process. Though they are yet to reach a shared decision on how to proceed with implementing the congregation's vision for ministry, they are well down the road in the discernment process. God's transforming perspective has been deeply introduced into the discussion, and the active engagement of the struggle among the council members to move this perspective into practice is under way.

This process assumes the presence of the Spirit to lead and guide a congregation, through its leaders, into discerning the will of God in relation to its particular context and into making strategic choices to implement this understanding. The Spirit's leading involves the gifts of all God's people. These diverse gifts, with their inherent multiple perspectives, contribute to the communal character of discernment and decision making.

Understanding Assumptions from the State Church Model

One of the main challenges facing most congregations of mainline denominations is that they tend to be locked into an institutional model of the church that is patterned after the state churches of Northern Europe. The state church is what is often referred to as the established church or Constantinian Christendom model of church.[1] It makes several assumptions that did not translate well into the free-church approach to congregational life and denominational formation that emerged within the American colonies in the seventeenth and eighteenth centuries.

The established state church assumed, first of all, that the culture was supportive of the church and the Christian message. Second, it assumed that everyone in the empire was Christian—if you were born into the parish, you were baptized into the local parish church.

This meant that any imagination for a mission field was defined as being somewhere beyond the boundaries of the empire. Third, the church existed primarily to serve the needs of its own members and to provide them with the religious goods and services that they expected to receive as members. Fourth, this church was financed through a system of state-led taxation that tended to diminish members having an active concern for stewardship within their local parish. Fifth, this church assumed that a pastor was a pastor, was a pastor—meaning that ordained leaders could be viewed largely as a system of interchangeable parts. It became clear that this approach to church needed to be altered to fit the realities encountered by the church in the American colonies and the newly formed United States.

While various changes were made to help the church adjust to the new conditions in the United States, many congregations and their denominations continue to be deeply influenced by assumptions that have been carried over from the established state-church pattern. Such congregations understand membership to merit certain rights and privileges in providing a variety of religious goods and services. These congregations focus primarily inwardly, serving the needs of members, and they expect to be respected and valued by the broader culture, even though the culture has become increasingly secular and even hostile toward the church. Finally, these congregations have difficulty envisioning their own larger community and local context as a mission field.

Understanding and Addressing the Age Gap

Another challenge that most congregations of mainline denominations are facing is the huge age gap that exists between their members
and the population at large. For example, while the average age of the
American population is now about thirty-eight, the ELCA reports that
fifty-three (or older) is the average age of membership in their 10,400
congregations. That's a gap of fifteen years! This helps to explain the
dramatic decline in the number of children in most of our congregations. We simply have not continued to reach even our own adult
children who are now bearing their own children, let alone reach the
significant number of younger families who are part of the general
population.

When looking at the aging of our congregations, it is also helpful
to note research that has been conducted on the differences in church
membership patterns among the various generations. According to
research conducted by George Barna and the Gallup organization,
about 65 percent of the Traditionalists, or Builders as they are sometimes called (the generation born before 1946), consider themselves
active members of a Christian based faith community in the United
States, while only 35 percent of the Baby Boomers (those born between
1946 and 1964) consider themselves to be so. However, the track record
with the younger generation is dismal and shocking, with only 10 percent of Generation X, also known as the Buster Generation (those born
between 1965–1983), and 4 percent of the Millenialists (those born
after 1983), who represent the current crop of high school and college
age youth, identify with any formal Christian congregation.[2]

Given these realities, it should not be surprising that the older
generations in most congregations define church primarily as a place
where they expect to be spiritually fed and to have their needs met.
This is what might be referred to as a "chaplaincy model" of church. It
is a model that continues to reflect many of the values inherited from
the established state church pattern. The younger generations are
increasingly finding this kind of church irrelevant to their quest for
spirituality, a spirituality that touches their daily lives and that is able

to impact life in their community. Their vision of the church is not that of a social club that tends to focus primarily inward on the needs of members. In contrast, they are interested in a more activist, missional approach to church life that takes Christian discipleship seriously and that helps them live out their faith in the world—becoming effective ambassadors for Christ.

The biggest challenge seems to be helping those in the older generation—those who make up the majority of the members and often provide much of the financial support in our congregations—cultivate a more missional vision. The question stands: "How might those who are comfortable with the church as it is be invited into discovering that the church needs a complete makeover?" Clearly there is a necessary and legitimate role for the church to play in caring for the needs of its members. But this should not become an end in itself. God's intent was always for this to serve as a means to a greater end—a fuller participation by the church in God's mission in the world. It is imperative that transformational leaders lift up a larger, missional vision for a congregation to serve as a *discipling community*. In his book *Beyond Maintenance to Mission*, Craig Nessan writes, "The number one priority for Christian education in our time is disciple-making. . . . This priority contributes to the fundamental purpose of the congregation, building Christian identity for the sake of Christ's mission in the world."[3]

The Congregation as a Discipling Community

The missional congregation finds its purpose grounded in God's mission—living for the sake of the world as it participates in God's redemptive ministry of reconciliation for all creation. Within this identity people are invited to make life-changing commitments as they discover the grace of God in becoming modern-day disciples of Jesus Christ. The missional congregation understands baptism as a call to vocational service of God and others; an ordination into ministry in daily life. The missional congregation is serious about cultivating committed disciples for Jesus instead of just adding more members to the institutional church.

Congregations that focus on *discipleship* are:

- not as concerned about numbers; and more concerned with how well people are living their faith and sharing the gospel.
- not as concerned about how well we care for members; and more concerned with how we serve needs in the world around us.
- not as concerned about maintaining institution (structure); and more concerned with empowering people for ministry.
- not as concerned about preserving facilities (ownership); and more concerned with offering them as a gift to our community.

What if congregations in the United States were to rediscover their purpose as discipling communities? What if every congregation reordered its priorities for ministry with the primary focus of helping these communities of faith grow in their relationship with Jesus Christ in order to live out a discipleship that was for the sake of the world? This is the challenge that faces us on our quest to become a missional church that takes to heart Jesus' command to "go and make disciples" (Matt. 28:19).

One congregation's purpose statement proclaims: "*Being and making passionate disciples for Jesus Christ through the power of the Holy Spirit.*" This congregation knows it is not enough to go and make disciples without first learning how we are to become disciples ourselves. There are three elements to growing and making disciples according to Jeff Jones in his book *Traveling Together: A Guide for Disciple-forming Congregations.* In order to grow as disciples, he suggests there needs to be regular experiences of deepening, equipping, and ministering.

According to Jones, "Deepening is about relationships—with God, self, and others." [4]

The foundational relationship of all disciples is with God in Jesus Christ. In addition, an awareness of one's self is also a growing relationship for the disciple, especially in discovering one's gifts and abilities. The third dimension of deepening is growth in relationships with others as a community. Becoming faithful disciples requires that we become deeply engaged in a local community of faith.

"Equipping is about preparation."
This has two dimensions. The first relates to our gifts and call. The second deals with skills and knowledge. Discovering and nurturing God's gifts helps disciples come to an understanding of their call in relation to ministry. Developing skills and knowledge, where disciples come to know certain things, equips them to do certain things.

"Ministering is about involvement."
Ministry is the participation of disciples in God's mission of redeeming all creation. The gifts disciples have, the call they receive, and the skills and knowledge they acquire are put to use through engaging in actual ministry. God's intent is for this to happen both inside and outside the church.

The Marks of Discipleship

Becoming disciples is a lifelong process that begins with baptism. In baptism, God claims us and marks us forever with the cross of Jesus Christ. In baptism, we are set aside for covenant living. A covenant is a mutual agreement or contract. God promises to be our God granting us the gifts of life, forgiveness, and salvation; and in affirming our baptism, we promise to live in God's grace as God's holy people. The words from the Affirmation of Baptism service give us an indication of what the life of a disciple includes.

> The pastor asks the candidate:
> You have made public profession of your faith. Do you intend to continue in the covenant God made with you in holy baptism:
> to live among God's faithful people,
> to hear the word of God and share in the Lord's supper,
> to proclaim the good news of God in Christ through word and deed,
> to serve all people, following the example of Jesus,
> and to strive for justice and peace in all the earth?[5]

The new pastor of Amazing Grace wanted to introduce the idea of disciple-making as a key element to becoming a missional congregation. He started with articles in the parish newsletter about what it means to be disciples, followers of Jesus in today's world. Then he preached a six-week sermon series on the six marks of discipleship as outlined in "Power Surge: Six Marks of Discipleship for a Changing Church," by Michael Foss.[6] Staff and congregational members were given small cards printed with the marks of discipleship to carry in their wallets and to refer to as needed.

We will strive to be passionate followers of Jesus Christ who . . .

Pray   *daily*

Worship   *weekly*

Read   *the Bible daily*

Serve   *at and beyond Amazing Grace Church*

Relate   *with others to encourage spiritual growth*

Give   *generously with a goal of 10% and beyond*

It is important to note that these marks of discipleship are not some new set of spiritual laws that we as a community of disciples must follow in order to earn God's favor. Practicing these Christian behaviors does not earn us special grace or heavenly brownie points. According to Foss, "They are simply habits of the soul that open us to the wonder and mystery of God's active presence in our lives. They keep us focused; they fix our attention on the things of God."[7] Christians practice these marks of discipleship out of a newfound commitment to Christ and the community of faith. When adopted and practiced regularly by members of a congregation, spiritual growth takes place. This spiritual growth also normally leads to numerical growth. This is the result of a community of God's people practicing a common commitment to discipleship that includes mutual support, encouragement, and reinforcement.

It is especially important that the leaders of a discipling community lead by example. Leaders must be intentional in their own spiritual growth as disciples as well as in maintaining the church's focus on disciple-making. With all the demands of church life, not to mention life in the world, it is easy to become distracted by other tasks or preoccupied by other models. Church consultant Bill Easum encourages church leaders to stay the course: "Leaders sense that the basic genetic code of the church is to *make disciples of Jesus Christ*, not to take care of people."[8]

Remember as leaders that you are also on a shared journey of discipleship with the community of believers that God has called you to lead. While leaders are busy leading and discipling others, they are also being formed as disciples of Jesus and are growing in their own gift and experience of God's grace. The marks of discipleship that shape your community of faith will also help mold you into the kind of disciples and leaders that God wants you to be. Make sure that, as leaders, you are practicing the six marks of discipleship—first of all collectively as a gathered group of leaders, and then also as individuals.

Church leader Jeff Jones offers several suggestions for ways to reshape a congregation's leadership team into a community of disciples.[9]

1. Encourage the council or committee to move away from a business-only approach to its work and become a spiritual community. Encourage the development of four new practices for church councils: telling personal faith stories, biblical reflection, prayerful discernment for making decisions, and visioning the future for planning.

2. Look at ways in which the work of the council encourages deepening, equipping, and ministering in the life of the congregation.

3. Do Bible studies on discipleship. Being exposed to biblical accounts of discipleship can help councils better understand their role in forming disciples.

4. Use the qualities or marks of discipleship to shape your own work as leaders.

5. Don't be afraid to let some programs that may have outlived their effectiveness die. This may allow a new ministry that is more timely to emerge and take flight.

6. Continue to shape, interpret, and hold up a vision of disciple-making to the congregation. A leader cannot over communicate the vision.

The pastor at Amazing Grace Church shared his vision for disciple-ship with his staff and lay leaders. He shared how God had opened his eyes to seeing the church as an equipping center for disciples—where people would grow in their faith, discover their gifts, and learn new skills for living out their faith in their daily life. But what would they call this new ministry of discipleship? One of the leaders then related a story of seeing a minivan advertising someone as a personal fitness trainer and wondered if the congregation might become known as a spiritual fitness center! This concept was adopted with enthusiasm and became a "tagline" to promote the new purpose and vision of the congregation to the larger community. It was determined that this would be a way to keep the vision of disciple-making in front of the membership at all times. And with the popular emphasis on physical fitness among the general public, this would also be a means of effec-tively communicating and connecting with the larger community.

Discipleship is all about helping God's people connect their faith and their gifts with God's mission in the world. Discipleship doesn't stop at the doors of the church; it isn't concerned only with what goes on inside a congregation. Rather, the focus of the congregation is on strengthening the community of faith for service in God's mission in the world. Discipleship is about bearing witness to the kingdom of God by pursuing truth, justice, mercy, peace, and love in the world.

Theologian Frederick Buechner said, "The place God calls you to is the place where your deep gladness and the world's deep hunger meet."[10] Discipleship is about equipping God's people to be a channel of grace through which God can mend a broken world. Discipleship is a journey worth everything we have.

 ## Discovery Questions

1. How would you explain the Spirit's ministry of spiritual transformation in light of the teaching of Romans 12? How does this inform the ministry of becoming a discipling community?

2. How would you describe the difference between a maintenance congregation and a missional congregation? Describe and discuss your congregation's present ministry in light of this contrast?

3. What is the difference between a membership approach and a discipleship approach to being the church? How are these informed by the Bible and by church history?

4. What would it take for your congregation to become a discipling community? What are some first steps that might be taken?

Resources for the Journey

Foss, Michael. *Power Surge: Six Marks of Discipleship for a Changing Church*. Minneapolis: Augsburg Fortress, 2000.

Hammett, Edward and James Pierce. *Reaching People Under 40 While Keeping People Over 60: Being Church for All Generations*. St. Louis: Chalice, 2007.

Jones, Jeffrey. *Traveling Together: A Guide for Disciple-forming Congregations*. Herndon, Va.: Alban Institute, 2006.

McClaren, Brian. *Church on the Other Side: Exploring the Radical Future of the Local Congregation*. Grand Rapids, Mich.: Zondervan, 2005.

Nessan, Craig. *Beyond Maintenance to Mission: A Theology of the Congregation*. Minneapolis: Augsburg Fortress, 1999.

Cultivate a Healthy Climate

A new contemporary worship service was being planned for the fall at Amazing Grace Church. Many youth and young families had requested that this be considered as an alternative to the regular, more traditional Sunday worship. And so this was one of the objectives included in the congregation's five-year strategic plan. However, adding a new service to the Sunday schedule meant moving nine o'clock worship up a half hour to 8:30 to allow time for Sunday school between services. The new contemporary service would be offered at 10:45.

A few older members began to complain about having to come half an hour earlier on Sunday in order to attend the traditional worship service. One woman was especially vocal in her protest when confronting Carol, the congregational president.

"It just doesn't seem right that those of us who have been faithful members should have to come to church earlier on Sundays to attend the service that we like."

"It seems like a hardship to have to adjust your personal schedule on Sunday?" Carol inquired.

"Well, it does take some of us older folk a while to get going in the morning, you know. Why can't the contemporary service be held at an earlier time and let us come later?"

"We've done some research on that, and it seems that the youth and visitors that might be interested in a contemporary service are

more likely to come at a later hour. So you might think of it this way: by coming a half hour earlier on Sunday, you are making a seat available at 10:45 for someone else to hear the gospel."

"I never thought of it that way. I guess that's important, isn't it? I can come early."

There are two lessons here. One is that the congregational president was able to re-frame the issue and turn it into a missional question. While taking a parishioner's concern seriously, she helped her understand the reason and value of the change. In the past, a church leader might have become defensive and further raised the anxiety level of the person with a concern. Another valuable lesson was learned when the congregational president shared this incident with the church council. The pastor commended her and urged all the council members to follow her example. "Let's all be on the same page," he suggested, "so that all of us can be a non-anxious presence when addressing concerns and questions that people may have. Let's keep the focus on our mission." The clear premise here is that healthy, Spirit-led leaders can bring about healthy change and transformation.

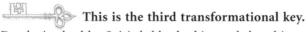 **This is the third transformational key.**
Developing healthy, Spirit-led leadership can help cultivate a positive climate change within the faith community.

Beginning the Journey of Transformation

Any journey of transformation starts with the leadership of a congregation. Leaders come in many shapes and sizes, ordained and lay, congregational staff and members. Some are quiet and reflective. Others are gregarious and intense. According to seminary professors Norma Cook Everist and Craig Nessan, all leaders are called to a ministry of transformation "that guides the people of God, helping them fulfill their calling and purpose. Leaders help to organize the church so that maximum use is made of all its resources, motivating people to work for the renewal of church and world. Leadership—grounded in trust in God, liberated by the love of Christ, and empowered by the Spirit—gathers, nurtures, teaches, and inspires the church to be the gifted people of God in mission."[1]

This chapter will explore the critical role of healthy, Spirit-led leadership as the agents of healing and transformation. Both clergy and lay leaders have a stake in cultivating healthy congregations, which at times includes restoring health and wholeness to broken congregations. They are called to lead a congregation creatively and successfully through times of crisis and change. Healthy, Spirit-led leaders can also help guide a congregation to new heights of participation in God's mission in their larger community and in the world.

Cultivating a Climate Change

Because of changes in the larger communities congregations serve as well as within congregations themselves, conflicts may arise with competing groups vying for power. When left unaddressed, congregations run the risk of becoming dumping grounds for all sorts of toxic feelings. It is natural that people bring their personal problems and unhealthy habits with them into the church. But when these patterns are left unchecked they contribute to congregational dysfunction. Like every organization based on relationships, the church tends to operate as a type of family system.[2] Healthy and unhealthy people are part of the system, and the actions of each individual affect the whole. Unresolved issues—many of which were swept under the rug only to reappear in other forms—poison the climate. Israel Galindo writes about this in her insightful book, *The Hidden Lives of Congregations*:

At the heart of much of what troubles congregations today is a continued failure to understand the corporate nature of congregational relationships and the underlying, often invisible, dynamics at play therein. In the press of day-to-day ministry and periodic conflict, clergy and congregational leaders tend to deal only with surface issues and symptoms. This leads to a reactive, rather than a proactive approach to ministry and congregational leadership. Lacking awareness of the underlying dynamics of congregational life, leaders cannot provide vision, manage crisis, or move a congregation from being stuck to moving forward.[3]

So what does it take to help a congregation get unstuck and move forward? What resources are available to encourage thinking as a missional church? What capacities has the Spirit of God built into the very *being* of the missional church? In the coming pages we will look at two impulses that inform how the Spirit of God is at work in the missional church.

The Missional Church as Always Forming and Reforming

Too often, established congregations resist change even when trying something different would enhance their ministry. On the other hand, new and developing congregations often ignore key aspects of the historic Christian faith in an effort to become more relevant to a new generation. In the first case, congregations fail to recontextualize their identity within a changing context. In the second, congregations over-contextualize their identity in trying to relate to the larger community. Both approaches fall short of the inherent ministry capabilities of the Spirit-created and Spirit-led missional church.

It is crucial to understand that the Spirit has created the missional church to always be both *reforming* (reclaiming essential biblical and theological truths) and *forming* (responding to new and changing contexts). The former inherent impulse was emphasized during the Protestant Reformation around the concept that the *church is always reforming* (*ecclesia semper reformanda*). This important insight needs to be complemented, however, by the other inherent impulse of the Spirit-led missional church which is that the *church is always forming* (*ecclesia semper formanda*).

This is the deeper truth about the missional church and the ministry of the Spirit that needs to be cultivated in the imagination of congregations. This understanding creates a dynamic and healthy tension between maintaining continuity while responding creatively to change.

Amazing Grace is faced with the challenge of stewarding its history of being a Lutheran congregation with a strong family-focused ministry, but doing so by translating this to a new generation of families. This new generation includes both younger Anglo families who are buying starter homes, but who have no historic connection with Amazing Grace, as well as the upwardly mobile Hispanic families that are moving into the area.

The reason the Spirit-led missional church pursues both of these strategies—always forming and reforming—is that this is part of its very nature. It carries within its DNA both the passion to engage the new while stewarding a proper understanding of the old. How does this understanding inform healthy, Spirit-led leadership? What kind of leadership is needed to help a congregation successfully manage crisis and engage change? Let's continue our journey of discovery as we consider those characteristics, skills, and insights that we will find helpful as leaders of a congregation who desire to make a positive difference.

Leading in Times of Crisis and Change

Asking the pastor to resign or electing new lay leaders seems to be an all too common approach to solving a crisis and seeking to revitalize a struggling congregation. David Laubach asserts that many people think that "very few turnarounds take place without replacing most of the present leaders. It is usually unwise to think that the same people who got the church into its current mess can lead it out of the mess."[4] While this may be true in some cases—particularly where the level of conflict has escalated to the point that current leaders have lost all credibility and effectiveness—it is also true that simply changing horses midstream is not necessarily the answer either.

Might it be possible to change the church by transforming its leadership? While the old adage suggests that it is hard for old dogs to learn new tricks, we believe that God is still in the business of changing and transforming people. We believe that leaders reading this book desire to grow in understanding of what it means to be an effective leader. We also believe that God's Spirit is already in the process of opening your eyes to see new possibilities and recognize new, healthier ways of using your leadership gifts.

Ron Heifetz articulates a new style of leadership for today's fast-changing world. In *Leadership on the Line*, Heifetz and Marty Linsky speak of the need for leaders who can address adaptive change.[5] This type of change runs contrary to the common approach of pastoral and lay leaders who seek technical solutions like hiring new staff, implementing programs, or renovating facilities to problems. Adaptive change necessitates a fundamental rethinking of the core values of a congregation. Such change requires congregational leaders to invite others to participate in the life of the faith community, perhaps by adapting ministry to reach a multicultural constituency that now makes up the larger community, or by reframing worship to be multigenerational while attending to the diverse style preferences of the generations.

Moses is an example of a biblical leader who was called into adaptive leadership in a time of crisis and change. No one before Moses had led a million people on a journey out of Egypt and through the wilderness. He didn't have AAA to provide maps for the journey, or a catering company to provide food service. And Moses certainly didn't have books on leadership to consult. Moses faced uncharted territory. His was an adaptive change. He took what he knew and applied this knowledge in unfamiliar circumstances. Moses trusted God to show him the way, but he also listened to the voices of others, especially his father-in-law, Jethro (Exodus 18). Moses and the children of Israel set out on a quest that became a journey. Healthy, Spirit-led leaders of congregations on their own journeys of transformation can learn much from Moses' example of adaptive change.

Leaders that learn to engage in *adaptive change* understand that such change isn't about implementing the right programs, following a specific formula, having the right answers, or developing the correct organizational structure. These are all helpful in addressing technical needs, but adaptive leadership means learning a range of practices that can be engaged with flexibility and creativity in changing contexts and in different situations. Leadership in this sense is an art where leaders summon forth originality and creativity, as one seeks to serve as God's transforming agent for the sake of the church and the world.[6]

The Spirit-Led Practice of Conveying a Non-Anxious Presence

Amazing Grace Church had experienced a great deal of trauma following the resignation of a beloved pastor and the resulting exodus of good staff and church members. Looking for someone to blame for their unhappy state, some members of the congregation pointed the finger at the elected lay leadership while others placed the blame at the feet of the bishop and synod staff. Trust was at an all-time low. As a result, members were suspicious of congregational leadership, expecting that someone might be trying to pull a fast one.

People vary in their level of maturity and experience in how to deal with a difficult situation. Those on the lower end of the scale tend to be more *reactive,* quick to blame and to criticize. They are impatient in finding a solution and often want a quick fix to the problem. They tend to focus on others, and have a hard time seeing that they are part of the problem and thus also need to be part of the solution. They frequently fail to take ownership for their concerns. Rather than using personal statements ("this is what I think or feel"), they are apt to say something like: "I understand that many people are upset about this."

A healthy, Spirit-led leader is one who has learned how to be *responsive* to diverse situations, even when unanticipated. This type of leadership is more reflective and thoughtful. They use the thinking part of the brain, not just those parts that deal with emotions or survival instincts.[7] They are able to stand back from a situation and observe with some objectivity what is really going on. They take responsibility for their statements, and are more likely to recognize when they may be part of the problem. They learn to work at not taking things personally, and are often more patient in trying to work out a more long-term and lasting solution.

Congregational consultant Peter Steinke commends leaders who exhibit what he calls a "non-anxious" presence. In his excellent book, *Congregational Leadership in Anxious Times*, Steinke writes: "The leader's capacity to be in conscious control over (to respond to) automatic functioning (reaction) affects the well-being of the whole community. The leader's 'presence' can have a calming influence on reactive behavior. Rather than reacting to the reactivity of others, leaders with self-composure and self-awareness both exhibit and elicit a more thoughtful response."[8]

Steinke likes to speak of healthy leaders as part of an *immune system* that helps keep disease in check. If a leader becomes anxious or defensive when approached by a member of the congregation who is upset about a particular situation, the leader unwittingly acts as a carrier in the spread of the disease and contributes to a rise in the level of anxiety experienced in that community of faith. On the other hand, as we saw in the scenario that opened this chapter, leaders like Carol who respond in a Spirit-led, non-anxious way can help lower the anxiety level considerably and actually diffuse issues.

Getting Started

Consider the possibility for a climate change in your congregation. What are some things that need to be changed to make your congregation a healthier, more Spirit-led community of faith? What would it mean to be a congregation led in the power of the Holy Spirit to participate more fully in God's mission in its ministry context, rather than expending time and energy on internal conflicts?

Kelly Fryer suggests there are five strategic behaviors that can effect change and also enable a congregation to become the church God intends it to be.

> A congregation that knows its purpose is to equip and empower people to be the kind of church God needs *out there* will be a congregation where people engage in five strategic behaviors:
> - get focused
> - set people free
> - take action
> - expect surprises
> - be hopeful.[9]

Let's examine each of these behaviors and explore how your congregational leadership might adapt them to your particular situation. Take some liberty with these categories as you think about cultivating a climate change in your congregation.

Getting Focused

Getting focused is about getting in touch with God's will for your ministry. It includes searching God's word together and joining in holy conversation about the mission and purpose of your congregation. As leaders, it will be important for you to interpret God's mission and your congregation's purpose, as well as to continue to lift up a vision for ministry for the congregation. You can help sustain a healthy climate by staying focused on your missional identity, your common purpose, and your shared vision (see chapter one).

Set People Free

Set people free by speaking the truth in love. Jesus said "you will know the truth, and the truth will make you free" (John 8:32). Leaders are to be truth-tellers, and should not be afraid to confront people in a loving way, to state the brutal facts, or to name the hard realities. We can only expect the climate to change when we are truthful with each other. This frees people to focus not on the problem but on God's mission!

Take Action

Take action. Be bold and courageous in doing so. The builders of the cathedral in Seville, Spain, give us a wonderful example of bold and courageous action. In 1401 these visionaries for the faith wrote: "Let us build here a church so great that those who come after us will think us mad ever to have dreamed it!"[10] What decisions might you be bold to consider in your life together as a congregation as you seek to carry out God's mission?

Expect Surprises

You can count on God to bring about positive change as you step forward with courage into the future that God has in store for your congregation. As adaptive leaders, you need to be able to respond creatively to surprises when they come, and you can expect surprises. Always remember, things usually do not go fully as planned. Adjustments often need to be made along the way. But in the midst of surprises, let your imagination explore what God might be wanting to do!

Be Hopeful

Finally, be hopeful. Some people will get on board right away with your congregation's missional plan. Others will be slower to come around. Some may resist the plan entirely and even attempt to sabotage the effort. Healthy, Spirit-led leaders learn to listen patiently to all concerns and adapt as necessary. But in the midst of this, they are also able to help people focus on God's mission and their congregation's purpose and vision while remaining hopeful about the outcome and knowing that God is ultimately in charge.

Discovery Questions

1. Why is it that congregations often seem to be so resistant in being able to adjust to changes in a timely manner?

2. What does it mean that the missional church is always both *forming* and *reforming*? How does this provide perspective for helping congregations respond to changes in their contexts and within their congregational life?

3. How does healthy, Spirit-led leadership function in facing major changes or crises? What are some practices they can engage in to help guide a congregation to respond redemptively?

4. If you were to do a diagnostic test on the present health of your congregation—both in terms of how people relate with each other and how effectively the congregation is participating in God's mission—how would you rate your congregation on a scale of one to ten (with one being the lowest and ten being the highest)? What are the implications of your score?

Resources for the Journey

Everist, Norma Cook and Craig Nessan. *Transforming Leadership: New Vision for a Church in Mission*. Minneapolis: Fortress Press, 2008.

Friedman, Edwin H. *Generation to Generation: Family Process in Church and Synagogue*. New York: Guilford, 1985.

Glaindo, Israel. *The Hidden Lives of Congregations: Discerning Church Dynamics*. Herndon, Va.: Alban Institute, 2004.

Heifetz, Ronald. *Leadership without Easy Answers*. Boston: Belknap Press of Harvard University Press, 1998.

Heifetz, Ronald A. and Marty Linsky, *Leadership on the Line: Staying Alive through the Dangers of Leading*. Boston: Harvard Business School Press, 2002.

Steinke, Peter. *Congregational Leadership in Anxious Times: Being Calm and Courageous No Matter What*. Herndon, Va.: Alban Institute, 2006.

6

Build a Supportive Team of Staff and Lay Leadership

In his state of the church address at a gathering of congregations from across the state, the bishop talked about the importance of fostering healthy churches that are open to the leading of God's Spirit and passionate about mission outreach.

"If 'mom' and 'pop' are on the same page," he announced, "the rebellious children in the congregation won't have a chance to make much trouble."

The bishop went on to explain that if church staff and lay leaders are united in their sense of mission and see themselves as supportive members of the same team, then they present an unbeatable force for change. When dissenters adverse to change see staff and leaders disagreeing or even sense division within the parish leadership, they seize the opportunity to stir the pot, adding to the anxiety already present in the congregation.

A healthy team consists of church leaders—both paid and volunteer—who view themselves as partners in ministry and are empowered to use their gifts and skills in order to further the missional goals of the congregation.

This is the fourth transformational key.
*It is imperative that care and intentionality be taken to build
a supportive, missional leadership team that is comprised of
both staff and lay leaders.*

Developing a Missional Leadership Team

It is important that congregations learn not to depend on one particular leader to either *save* them or *restore* their church to its former
glory. A more missional and vital future is ensured when a variety of
leaders are called forth with their many and varied gifts to form a gen-
uine partnership for the sake of helping the congregation participate
in God's mission in the world. This team of missional leaders needs
to be comprised of both the called staff of a congregation and the
elected leadership of the congregation. They need to be persons who
understand the importance of supporting each other as they carry out
their mutual ministry in the church and in the larger community and
the world. Keeping God's perspective in view is foundational if this is
to occur.

God's Plan and Missional Congregations

The primary way God's people exist in the world today is in the form
of congregations. Congregations are at the center of God's plan and
purpose. They bear witness through the Spirit to the reconciling
power of God through Christ in their own midst and to the larger
community in which they minister. What this means is that congregations are unique. They represent God in the world, being formed by
the Spirit as particular communities that live in dynamic relationship
with their larger communities. This perspective stands at the core of a
congregation's identity. A congregation needs to understand itself as
being a community created by the Spirit. It needs to understand itself
as being a community where persons live in reconciled relationship
with one another through the power experienced in Christ's death
and resurrection. It needs to understand itself as being a community

that bears witness to the world that God desires all of life to be reconciled through Christ to the living God (2 Cor. 5:16-21). It needs to understand that it is a community that by its very nature is called, formed, and sent to participate in God's mission within its immediate community as well as in the larger world.

Congregations Enact God's Ministry of Reconciliation in the World

As discussed in chapter two, congregations have a dual nature. They are both human and holy. They have very concrete and particular aspects that contribute to their identity. Also embedded in their identity is their involvement in the creation-wide work of God in the world. It's crucial for congregations to comprehend that God's love extends to the world through diverse congregations, each within a unique context. In fact, in the work of creation and redemption, God uses particular human communities to make God's purposes clear within the contexts in which they serve.

This manner of God at work in the world is seen most clearly in the incarnation. In Jesus, God took on human flesh (John 1:14), becoming concrete in order to make redemption available to all people in every time and place. Jesus' humanness as a Jew living in Palestine under Roman domination did not limit the reach of redemption that Jesus accomplished for the entire world. The universal validity of redemption was made available within and through the particularity of Jesus being a Jew within the nation of Israel.

Amazing Grace is being called to see its changing community from God's perspective. This includes studying and responding to the changing demographics of age, ethnicity, and mobility. It also includes enacting God's love within this context in ways that bring diverse people into reconciled relationships.

Congregations are created to participate in God's mission. They do not belong to themselves. They belong to God. As such, congregations are critical to God's work in the world. The primary way people come to learn about and experience the reconciling love of God is by encountering the people who make up a specific congregation. The primary way that reconciliation is enacted in the world is through people in congregations, like Amazing Grace, becoming involved in showing mercy, promoting justice, and sharing the good news of God's story with others. And these points serve as the basis for developing a missional leadership team that is able to support a common purpose and shared vision.

Creating Community among Staff

A healthy ministry climate is sustained and nurtured in large part by a healthy, Spirit-led staff who are supportive of one another and of the congregation's purpose. It is important that all staff members enter into a covenant of mutual trust and respect for one another. Part of this covenant involves serious and honest discussion about expectations and commitments that staff have, and make, for one another. Carefully defined job descriptions and clear lines of accountability help assure healthy working relationships. Equally important for a healthy, Spirit-led team is knowing that each member can count on the others to provide ongoing support and encouragement.

"We need to remember that we can agree to disagree in private, but we always need to be on the same page in public," the senior pastor told his staff. "We must always be openly supportive of each other if we are to ensure the health and mission of this parish." He explained: "I know of too many ministries that have been sabotaged because some member or members of a church staff aired their concerns with members of the congregation or allowed themselves to get sucked into a conflicted situation."

Staff members listened intently as the pastor shared several examples of how staff in other churches had allowed themselves to become triangulated in unhealthy ways with someone who had a vendetta against the pastor or other member of the team. In one case, a youth director, who was insecure about his own job, found himself agreeing with a parishioner who was berating one of the pastors. Rather than encouraging this disgruntled individual to go directly to the person they were upset with, the youth director commiserated with the unhappy member, which only added fuel to the fire. Eventually the youth director, now viewed as an ally by those who were displeased with the pastor, was drawn into the midst of the conflict and found himself siding with those who wanted to get rid of the pastor. When the pastor resigned, the youth director discovered that his job was now in jeopardy as well since the congregation, in choosing to embrace a climate of disagreement and disappointment, lost their focus on mission.

Staff development is another key to healthy team ministry. Staff members need to spend intentional time together in Bible study and prayer—praying for each other, for members of the congregation, and for God's mission in the world. Regular, weekly staff meetings are important to ensure good communication among team members. To be effective, these meetings should be mandatory for all full and part time staff. An agenda for staff meetings might include opening devotions, which staff members may take turns providing, lifting up mission highlights, and ministry updates shared by every member of the staff. It is also helpful to hold staff retreats on a regular basis, at least annually. Retreats allow time for staff to focus on spiritual formation and skill building, as well as a review of congregational purpose and vision, and working together on planning and goal setting.

The demands of ministry can take its toll on church staff. Therefore, it is good to provide a nurturing climate that affirms and values each member of the team. This can be done in a variety of ways. Team members should:

- Stay aware of how fellow teammates are doing and offer personal support.
- Gather on a regular basis for fellowship and mutual caring.
- Use a Mutual Ministry Team to provide additional support.[1]

Creating Community among Lay Leaders

Equally crucial to the health of a congregation's mission and ministry is the building of a healthy, Spirit-led team of elected lay leaders who are supportive of one another and of the congregation's purpose. There should be an expectation that the members of a leadership team will behave maturely and respectfully and will cooperate with one another for the good of the whole. Later in this chapter we will look at the explicit characteristics of healthy, Spirit-led leaders who are able to help create and sustain a healthy ministry climate.

Lay leaders are partners in ministry with church staff as well as with other members of a congregation. It is good for all elected leaders to see themselves as being valued and vital members of the church leadership team. Cultivating this should incorporate many of the same suggestions noted above regarding the building of a healthy staff team. Clear expectations and lines of accountability also need to be defined. Some congregations develop guidelines for their elected leaders similar to the following example.

$$\diamondsuit$$

Expectations for
Council Members and Other Church Leaders

But speaking the truth in love, we must grow up in every way into him who is the head, into Christ, from whom the whole body, joined and knit together by every ligament with which it is equipped, as each part is working properly, promotes the body's growth in building itself up in love. (Eph. 4:15-16)

1. A church leader is to be diligent in the use of the means of grace and of prayer. This means that one is to set an example by being regular in worship attendance.

2. A church leader is committed to helping fulfill the congregation's vision for mission.

3. A church leader supports the ministry of the congregation through regular giving—by practicing good stewardship in the sharing of time, talent, and treasure.

4. A church leader seeks to grow in one's own spiritual life by daily prayer and regular study of God's Word.

5. A church leader will show oneself to be dependable by regular attendance of scheduled meetings and following through on assigned responsibilities.

6. A church leader will exhibit a spirit of cooperation and collaboration by seeking to work together "for the common good" with staff and members of the congregation.

7. A church leader will seek to communicate clearly with other leaders, staff, and members of the congregation, seeking to avoid misunderstandings and to keep others informed.

8. A church leader respects the need for confidentiality in appropriate circumstances.

Leadership structures in the congregation, whether a church council or a ministry team, often function like small groups, incorporating time for *caring, spiritual nurture, mission focus,* and *action* into every meeting. At the beginning of each meeting people are asked to share what's going on in their lives and ministry. If people feel listened to and cared for, they are better able to set aside personal issues and get to the business at hand. Caring time may be followed by Bible study or devotions, reminding the group they are about God's work. This is also an opportunity for members to be nurtured in their own faith. Next the pastor or another key leader can offer a few reflections that reference God's mission and the congregation's purpose and vision. This helps the group to maintain a strategic perspective, one that focuses on their enacting God's ministry of reconciliation within the life of the congregation and the larger community they serve. It also allows them to continue to utilize their missional plan as a template for all of their decision-making. Finally, the group is compelled to action—finding ways to implement their purpose and vision in pursuing their missional goals.

When a church council adopts a format based on such a small-group approach to the functioning of governance structures, some council members can be nervous about including all four components, recalling that meetings often used to last as long as three or more hours. To everyone's amazement, when using the new format many councils find they are able to conduct their business within two hours and usually finish in less time. Below is a typical timetable that has proven to be successful for many councils.

Sample Council Agenda

7:00–7:15: Members meet in small groups for check-in

7:15–7:30: Bible study and opening prayer

7:30–7:45: Mission Teaching Moment (usually led by pastor)

(Usually references God's mission and the congregation's purpose and vision in some way)

7:45–8:00: Approval of Minutes and Reports

(This time is for clarification questions only since all information is submitted ahead of time as written reports)

8:00–8:30: Old and New Business

8:30: Members meet in small groups to pray for each other before leaving

Sometimes a faith community makes the mistake of tolerating for too long the inappropriate and disrespectful actions of a trouble-making parishioner or group. When people are given free rein to destroy a climate of trust and make a pastor or other leader the scapegoat, members of the church council need to have the courage to say: *This must stop! This is not helpful and is distracting us from our participation in God's mission.*[2] Unhealthy individuals or groups are often granted extraordinary power and control when their inappropriate behavior is left unchecked or church leaders find themselves spending an inordinate amount of time dealing with them and their issues. Rather, leaders would do well to invest most of their energies in building up the positive leadership traits in others and finding creative ways to advance God's mission through their congregation.

Healthy, Spirit-led leadership helps to cultivate a *permission-giving* climate that helps unleash the gifts of *all* God's people. Rather than being a church that narrowly controls who makes decisions about which ministries are permitted, missional leaders encourage all members to recognize their gifts and passion for ministry and affirm and support them. This approach multiplies and empowers new leaders for mission, and celebrates the priesthood of all believers, one of the central themes of the Reformation. Consider the following illustration of how this works.

A man wanted to start a weekend "soup kitchen" using the new commercial kitchen recently built by his congregation. He was a chef at a local restaurant and had many connections with food service businesses in the area. Under the old paradigm of control, the church council could have killed the man's enthusiasm by asking him to get approval from various parish groups. However, in a permission-giving climate, the leadership applauded the man's dream and, noting that this venture conformed to the congregation's purpose and vision for ministry, asked him to invite others, including the social concerns team, to join him in the effort.

Marks of Healthy, Spirit-Led Leadership

What are the characteristics of Spirit-led leadership who are able to promote a healthy, missional climate in a congregation? In his *Healthy Congregations* training program, Peter Steinke explores seven habits of such health-promoting leaders.[3]

Spiritual Grounding

Tending to one's faith and relationship with God helps one act responsibly as a missional leader. Secure in the knowledge of God's grace and acceptance, healthy, Spirit-led leadership is able to be responsive to the needs and concerns of others without getting defensive. These leaders live out their baptismal calling to serve God and others.

Manages Own Anxiety

Healthy, Spirit-led leaders are self-aware and know their own anxiety triggers. At the same time, they are able to take steps to control their own anxiety and not let it *infect* others. Such leadership practices a less anxious presence when dealing with other leaders and fellow members in the congregation.

Takes Positions and Stays Connected

Healthy, Spirit-led leaders practice the art of self-differentiation. Even while connecting with people and paying attention to their concerns, such leaders are able to keep a healthy distance and maintain a healthy perspective. They are also able to clearly articulate their position and take ownership for it. While respecting another's point of view, these leaders can say: "I appreciate that; now this is what I think."

Focuses on Presence and Functioning

Rather than getting caught up in the emotion of the moment, healthy, Spirit-led leadership is able to respond calmly and be present for the individual expressing a concern or question. "This is what I hear you saying. . ." is a way of letting a person know you hear them without agreeing with them. Another helpful response can be: "Here is where you can find out some more information about that issue."

Focuses on Vision and Mission

Healthy, Spirit-led leaders try to keep the focus of any conversation on God's mission and the congregation's purpose and vision in relation to this. There will be many temptations within congregational life for people to stray from that purpose and vision, and there will be many distractions that can sap a leader's energy. It is important to *stay the course* and maintain a sense of direction—of where the congregation is headed with its missional plan.

Focuses on Strengths

It is helpful to take stock of a congregation's assets—the resources of people, money, and facilities—because God has given Spirit-led leadership the responsibility to steward these for the sake of God's mission. While the temptation may be to focus on the weakness or growth areas of the congregation in proverbial "the glass is half empty" attitude, it is more productive to celebrate God's gracious gifts that provide for "the glass being half full"! This perspective is grounded in a theology of abundance that believes that God has given the congregation every gift it needs to accomplish God's mission in its particular context.

Challenges Self and Others

Healthy, Spirit-led leaders are aware of the pains and struggles in their own lives as well as in the lives of others. At the same time, they will not let this defeat or define them. Rather, they will rise above it with God's help. These people practice the art of collaboration and empowerment, always challenging themselves and other members of the team to live into the fullness of the life that Christ calls us to.

A Healthy Climate

A healthy climate is fostered by a healthy, Spirit-led team of staff and lay leaders who provide an environment where all of the members of a congregation can grow and thrive. One can readily sense when a church culture is not healthy—ideas are stifled, relationships are tense, people are not hopeful about the future. On the other hand, one can also sense when a church is healthy and being Spirit-led by the joy, hope, and enthusiasm expressed by members who are fully engaged. Leaders have an awesome privilege and responsibility to help cultivate and nurture an environment of trust and openness, one that calls forth and celebrates the gifts of all God's people.

Discovery Questions

1. What are some of the ways in which the life and ministry of congregations can be sabotaged when there is discord or conflict among staff or lay leaders of a congregation?

2. What are the marks of healthy, Spirit-led leaders? Reflect on how these qualities are currently manifest among the leadership of your congregation. Where are their gaps that need to be addressed?

3. What is the primary value of intentionally cultivating a healthy, Spirit-led congregational team of staff and lay leaders? What is the pastor's role in this work?

4. What kind of leadership style is most conducive to building a supportive team?

5. What does a healthy, Spirit-led leadership team look like? How would you rate your current leadership team in relation to living out this missional style of leadership?

Resources for the Journey

Frazee, Randy. *The Connecting Church: Beyond Small Groups to Authentic Community*. Grand Rapids, Mich.: Zondervan, 2001.

Frost, Michael and Alan Hirsch. *The Shaping of Things to Come: Innovation and Mission for the 21st Century Church*. Peabody, Mass.: Hendrickson, 2003.

George, Carl. *The Coming Church Revolution: Empowering Leaders for the Future*. Grand Rapids, Mich.: Revell, Baker, 1994.

Hammett, Edward with James Pierce. *Reaching People Under 40 While Keeping People Over 60: Being Church for All Generations*. St. Louis: Chalice, 2007.

Jones, Jeffrey. *Traveling Together: A Guide for Disciple-forming Congregations*. Herndon, Va.: Alban Institute, 2006.

Stay the Course
When Facing Conflict

*You won't get a dime out of me for this debt reduction campaign!"
exclaimed Steve, a retired stock-broker. "I don't agree with some of
the proposed changes in our vision for ministry plan. It just won't be
the same church anymore."*

*The pastoral intern was aware that the disgruntled man had been
spreading his poisonous thoughts among his older friends at church,
but this passionate pronouncement was made at a men's breakfast
meeting and everyone was listening in.*

"Tell me what you are afraid of," the Intern calmly said.

*"Well, I know we need to get some new members in here to pay
the bills. But I don't see how making our church more child or youth
friendly will accomplish this end. We'll just have more kids running
around out of control."*

*"Did you know that we are about to receive thirty new people as
members?" The intern smiled as she went on to explain, "The majority
are young families without a church home and they have been looking
for a congregation like ours where they can raise their children."*

"Didn't know," replied Steve, chagrined. "Glad to hear it."

*The intern continued, "I've heard from some of your friends that
you have been pretty unhappy and that, among other things, you've
been criticizing our youth and family minister to several people. Have
you tried talking directly to him about some of your concerns?"*

"I don't think he would pay any attention to an old man like me."

"Give him a try. I think you'd find him very open to hearing your concerns and ideas. What isn't helpful is complaining or putting people down in public. Our pastor tells us that this is not how members of a healthy, Spirit-led congregation behave toward each other."

"Yes, I guess so," sighed Steve. Then he added, "You know I'd feel better if you would come with me to speak to our youth minister."

"I'd be happy to. I know that you love this church and I would invite you to be part of the solution rather than part of the problem. You have a lot of wisdom and gifts to share."

Conflict is often generated by change in congregations or in the larger communities they serve. But, as we've just seen, conflict can be diffused by confronting it head-on. The pastoral intern was wise to confront the member in a caring and timely way, speaking the truth in love. Developing healthy communication practices will go a long way to promoting a positive climate of trust that will enable a congregation to focus its energies outward on participating in God's mission rather than on internal squabbling.

This is the fifth transformational key.
It is important for healthy, Spirit-led leadership to stay the course when facing conflict by practicing truth telling as an opportunity for learning and growing together.

"We need to improve communication around here!" is a frequent mantra heard from church leaders and parishioners in a multitude of congregations. Some complain that they lack the information they need to make reasonable decisions at a meeting of the Church Council or at a congregational meeting. Unhelpful rumors will often fly across the phone lines, resulting in misinformation and half-truths. The absence of a healthy, intentional system of communication in many congregations has led people to joke about the amount of church business that gets done in the church parking lot.[1]

Conflict Is to Be Expected

It is not uncommon to hear people say, "We just want to be like the New Testament church." They usually have in mind some romanticized view of a church that lived in harmony while growing ever and ever deeper in love and unity. Unfortunately, this is not the church we encounter as the Christian movement began to spread in the first century within a variety of contexts and locations. It is evident that numerous differences quickly arose, leading to conflict between congregations, between groups within congregations, and between individuals. Examples of these conflicts can be found in various New Testament writings.

Complaint over Injustice—Acts 6

Widows who were from Gentile families within the new Christian community were being marginalized in the daily food distribution within the Jerusalem church. When a complaint was raised, it eventually led to additional leadership being appointed by the apostles to care for the daily distribution.

Competing Theological Differences in the Larger Church—Acts 15

Competing understandings of the gospel developed between the church in Jerusalem and the church at Antioch. To address this difference a gathering of apostles and other leaders, known as the Council of Jerusalem, was called. They debated and resolved the question of how the gospel was to be understood—salvation is by grace through faith and nothing else!

Competing Parties within a Congregation—1 Corinthians 1

For some reason, groups of believers in the congregation at Corinth engaged in party politics with each group vying for who would be the most prestigious. This competition lead to groups identifying with different key leaders of the church—Peter, Apollos, Paul, and so forth.

Turning Theology into Ideology—Galatians 5

A group of believers within the Galatian church wanted to require all Gentile converts to accept Judaism in order also to become Christians. This party consistently created difficulties for the new Gentile converts and was sharply confronted by Paul for beliefs and requirements that were contrary to the gospel.

Turning Personal Scruples into Requirements for Others—
1 Corinthians 8 and Romans 14–15

There were people within the church who held deep personal convictions about any number of issues—such as eating meat offered to idols—who wanted to impose these views on others. They were urged to avoid doing something that might cause a weaker believer to fall into sin. But it was also concluded that someone's personal scruples should not necessarily limit another person's freedom.

Failing to Address Moral Issues—1 Corinthians 5

The church at Corinth was inappropriately allowing a person to continue to live in deep immorality. This was left unchecked without congregational discipline. Paul called this congregation to account and required them to address this situation.

Deep Personal Disagreement—Acts 15:36-41

Paul and Barnabas developed a sharp difference of opinion over whether John Mark should accompany them on another mission journey. This led to a parting of ways between them, and there is no indication that this breach was ever resolved.

Congregational life in New Testament times certainly knew conflict. It's normal for congregations of every era to face conflict. The key issue is not *whether* a congregation will have conflict, but rather, *how* such conflict will be handled. Congregations need to develop capacity to engage in conflict. Healthy, Spirit-led leaders will attend to developing such capacity. We believe they will find it helpful to have a framework available for diagnosing what they are facing, one that can help provide both perspective and direction for engaging in the biblical practice of truth-telling.

Building Capacity to Engage Conflict

This chapter is largely about building capacity to help congregations respond redemptively when facing conflict. One of the keys in helping congregations to de-escalate a conflict situation and to develop a redemptive response is by creating a healthy communication system within the congregation. Another key is helping everyone learn how "to speak the truth in love" as Saint Paul admonishes Christians to do in his letter to the Ephesians (4:15–16). To begin with, pastors and lay leaders need to acknowledge any unhealthy communication patterns that have been established and tolerated in the past, and then they need to find ways to correct these patterns as they seek to create a new congregational culture characterized by openness and trust.

A Congregation's Whitewater Time

Research indicates that it is often three to five years into a new pastorate before a climate of trust with lay leaders, staff, and members of a congregation is developed. This can take even longer in a congregation that has experienced trauma or a serious conflict. To establish such a climate of trust usually requires a congregation to work through some type of *significant difference* that involves conflict. The irony is that many clergy will choose to leave a congregation and search for another call before this work is completed. This is reflected in the fact that the average tenure for pastors in the Evangelical Lutheran Church in America is around six to seven years. Some mainline denominations such as the United Methodists report an even shorter term of about three years.[2] Though mainline churches' appointment systems may not encourage pastors to stay for longer terms, why do pastors seem so ready to bail out after such a short time, especially when they face their first conflict of any importance?

Church consultants such as Carl George call the five-year mark in congregational life the "whitewater" period.[3] This is a time when the honeymoon with a new pastor is over. The image of the congregation being like a raft on a river is illustrative. The raft has floated downstream for some distance in relatively calm waters, but begins to encounter some serious rapids where whitewater is stirring all around. Numerous rocks and whirlpools, along with other dangerous perils, must now be faced. To gain perspective on how congregations and their leaders engage such periods of whitewater, it is helpful to understand something about the varying response patterns that people have to accepting change. This is useful for appreciating both the period of whitewater and in developing strategies for dealing with it. The following diagram lays out the typical response patterns within congregations when planned change has been introduced into its ministry.

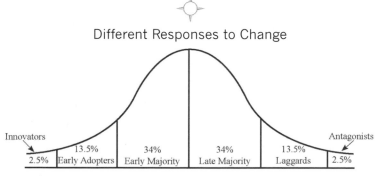

Different Responses to Change

Innovators · 2.5% · 13.5% Early Adopters · 34% Early Majority · 34% Late Majority · 13.5% Laggards · 2.5% · Antagonists

Modified from *Diffusion of Innovations*, Fifth Edition by Everett M. Rogers. Copyright © 1995, 2003 by Everett M. Rogers. Copyright © 1962, 1971, 1983 by The Free Press. All rights reserved. Reprinted with the permission of The Free Press, a Division of Simon & Schuster, Inc.

A number of people in a congregation are eager to embrace new leadership along with the changes it brings in order to move forward in ministry. The diagram indicates at least 50 percent of a congregation supports the leadership's direction within the first year or two. This includes a combination of people in the Innovators, Early Adopters, and Early Majority categories. Another 34 percent, the Late

Majority, will typically join in supporting a planned change within the first three years. They may offer some early resistance, but they usually modify their opinion about changes that are being made and come to accept them as the new reality. That leaves 16 percent, the combination of persons that might be described as Late Adopters and Laggards, who often dig in their heals and continue to resist the changes taking place. Unfortunately, it is not atypical for some of these folks, in their fight against change, to attempt to seize power and disrupt congregational ministry.[4] They will often generate conflict in order to get their way, which usually ends up throwing the ministry off track. Their behaviors can significantly increase the turbulence of whitewater that a congregation must go through.

It is during whitewater times that many pastors and other congregational leaders choose to jump ship by abandoning their call and their roles as leaders in the congregation. It is crucial that missional leaders remain on course and continue the quest. Change is inevitable, as is opposition to change. Conflict is predictable. As a wise person once said, "Life is change. Growth is optional. Choose wisely." The only recipe for healthy and redemptive growth is an intentional commitment to change.[5]

As leaders, we continue to engage the quest and take the journey in the knowledge that God's Spirit is leading us. We also know that this is the way that we actually grow deeper in our faith and in our discipleship. Like all rafts going downstream in a river, congregations will eventually pass through the rough waters and once more enjoy a time of smooth journey. It is important to realize that congregations will encounter challenges and obstacles along the way, but, with God's help, Spirit-led leadership can steer the congregation safely through the rapids and into God's missional future.

Responding to Rumors and Conflict: Speaking the Truth in Love

A retired hospital chaplain and her spouse joined Amazing Grace Church at the same time the congregation was in the search process for a part-time visitation pastor. Because of her expertise in grief work, the retired chaplain volunteered to lead a new small group on grief and loss. A rumor soon began floating around the church office about the new members. The business manager, uncomfortable with what she had heard, approached the senior pastor.

"One of our staff," she began, "told me that a member of the parish was wondering if we are paying this retired chaplain to lead the new small group. This member also thought that the staff and the search committee might be doing an 'end-run' around the congregation—that they have already decided to offer her the position of visitation pastor."

The pastor groaned as his staff colleague continued. "Not only that, but he had heard that the retired chaplain's spouse has a gambling problem."

Taking a deep breath, the pastor replied, "None of those rumors is true. I suspect that this person is reacting to the way things used to be done around here. At the same time, this is exactly the kind of behavior we are trying to discourage. Rumors such as these are not only inappropriate, they can also be destructive. We need to encourage people to get their facts straight and not spread malicious gossip that will hurt others. Instead of focusing on negative innuendo, shouldn't we all be grateful for the wonderful gifts this new couple brings to our congregation?!"

The new senior pastor chose to use this example to inform the staff and lay leaders about what was happening. In an effort to transform the climate of the congregation, he confronted the rumors head on and used them as a teaching tool. At the staff meeting the following week, as well as at a quarterly meeting of ministry team leaders, the pastor put the rumor to bed. He wanted his team of staff and lay leaders to know the truth so that they could help dispel the rumor, if necessary. He also encouraged them to remind anyone who came to them with unfounded gossip that this was not helpful or appropriate. "We are trying to create a new climate of openness and trust. To do so, we should all work together to promote healthy communication and positive ways of relating to one another," he concluded.

Church leaders often encounter statements that begin with, "Someone said . . .," or worse yet, "Many people have expressed a concern about. . . ." While various reasons may be given for sharing anonymous information, this should be vigorously challenged if leaders hope to promote a healthy climate of open and honest communication. Unhealthy behaviors such as rumor, gossip, murmuring, and third-party complaints are significant ways of resisting attempts at change and good health in congregations.[6] Members need to be held accountable and take ownership for their own thoughts, feelings, and concerns.

Responsible leaders can help enact two primary practices that assist in disabling rumors and stopping third-party complaints. First, since secrecy is often part of the problem, healthy, Spirit-led leaders refuse to keep secrets. Instead, they name and address unhealthy behavior. It is good to confront an individual offender directly, doing so out of concern and love for that person and the church community. Second, rumors, secrets, and anonymous complaints can be disabled by refusing to pass them on or perpetuate them. On the one hand, we can contain them by exposing inappropriate behavior, and on the other, we can provide accurate information about a situation and how decisions are made.

Communication Tools for a Healthy, Spirit-Led Congregation

There is a humorous story about a pastor who decided to preach on sin. Two older women who always sat in the front pew under the pulpit were hanging on his every word. As he railed against various wrongs people commit—robbery, murder, and adultery among them—the women were overheard saying "preach it to them pastor!" But when the pastor began to speak about the evils of gossip, one woman turned to the other and said, "Now he's just meddling!"

Congregations can be debilitated by gossip and unwarranted accusations. In addressing this, pastors and key lay leaders have the authority and responsibility to manage the dissemination of information.

Some misuse this authority by exercising careful control over how information is shared, thus creating a culture where deception is possible. Information is censored to hide mistakes. Confidential material is sometimes leaked by someone abusing power. Or more innocently, because a good communication system is not in place, information is not shared fully and in a timely way. What can be done to overcome the damage done by poor communication patterns and enhance the way that leaders and members share information with one another?

There are a number of communication tools that can be helpful to the pastor and elected leadership of a congregation as they seek to build a climate of openness and trust. Healthy, Spirit-led leaders will help a congregation identify negative patterns of behavior and then exemplify redemptive and healthier ways of managing information that can effectively transform their community.

The Pastor

• We recommend that every pastor be in supervision of some kind. This could be a spiritual director, a coach, or a pastoral counselor whom the pastor might see on a monthly basis. With the help of another, clergy can identify their own patterns of communication, especially those patterns that may impair congregational functioning.

• The pastor can use the "tools of the trade" to promote and enhance good communication and information sharing. Newsletter articles, sermons, and adult classes are all appropriate venues for the discussion of healthy communication patterns, and can also be a time for truth-telling. In addition, the pastor can lift up examples of good and helpful communication at church council meetings or ministry team meetings.

• The pastor also needs to exemplify good information sharing. Regular staff meetings and other team meetings are vital. At minimum, the pastor and the congregational president should have a regular monthly meeting. Likewise, effective use of various instruments of communication (such as e-mail, notes, and phone calls) is crucial to keeping everyone informed. A good rule of thumb is one can never communicate too much or too often!

The Elected Leadership

• Council meetings need to be open and transparent. Financial reports, minutes, and reports from staff and various ministry team leaders should be provided ahead of time. It is important that the elected leaders feel that they are "in the know" so they can help answer questions and be on the "same page" as advocates for the congregation's mission.

• Open forums are a good venue for sharing information and vetting questions and concerns about certain issues facing the congregation. A good practice is to plan a forum prior to every vote made by the congregation. If members have a chance to get adequate information and offer their input, they will feel that they are a part of the process and be able to make informed decisions.

• It is said that one needs to communicate the same information in at least five different ways. So when passing on information about what is happening in the congregation—particularly if you are planning any changes—it is good to use a variety of methods including temple talks, newsletter articles, group e-mails, the church Web site, posters, and bulletin inserts.

• When communicating something new to the congregation, such as a change in the vision for ministry plan, it is helpful to answer the following three questions: a) what will not change, b) what specifically is going to change and why, and c) how will this change enable us to better accomplish our missional plan as a congregation?

Communication in healthy, missional congregations needs to be transparent, open, and trustworthy. Leaders in these congregations *walk the talk* and invite people to follow their example. With courage and discernment, healthy, Spirit-led leaders are then able to navigate more successfully the whitewater that they encounter and lead their people on a journey of change and transformation.

Discovery Questions

1. Is there any evidence of discontent within your congregation at the present time? Are there any ways in which this discontent is playing out in ways that are not helpful?

2. How should congregations understand change and conflict in relation to the ministry of the Spirit in their midst? To what extent might conflict be referred to as being "biblical"?

3. Why are complaints and criticism used to express rising levels of anxiety in congregations? How should staff and leadership respond?

4. Why is it important to hold people accountable for their actions? What are some helpful practices for doing so?

Resources for the Journey

Boers, Arthur Paul. *Never Call Them Jerks: Healthy Responses to Difficult Behavior*. Herndon, Va.: Alban Institute, 1999.

Hanchey, Howard. *From Survival to Celebration: Leadership for the Confident Church*. Lanham, Md.: Cowley, 1994.

Laubach, David. *Twelve Steps to Congregational Transformation: A Practical Guide for Leaders*. Valley Forge, Pa.: Judson: 2006.

Leas, Speed B. *Moving Your Church through Conflict*. Herndon, Va.: Alban Institute, 1985.

Roxburgh, Alan and Fred Romanuk. *The Missional Leader: Equipping Your Church to Reach a Changing World*. San Francisco: Jossey-Bass, 2006.

Ruth, Kibbie Simmons and Karen A. McClintock. *Healthy Disclosure: Solving Communication Quandaries in Congregations*. Herndon, Va.: Alban Institute, 2007.

Practice Stewardship to Build Financial Viability

The business manager seemed flustered as she entered the pastor's office. "I don't know how we are going to make payroll again this month!" she said, almost sobbing.

"Sit down and tell me what's the matter," the pastor said, trying to console her.

"You know that we are currently operating with a deficit budget, which the congregation approved. While weekly attendance and giving is up since you arrived, it isn't enough for us to make ends meet and pay all our bills. I just don't know what to do."

"I've been concerned about this and know we have to get this congregation back on solid financial footing if we are to move forward with our new vision for ministry plan. I've asked our congregational president to call together some of the movers and shakers here at Amazing Grace. I'll ask them to help us come up with both a short-term solution to meet our current budget needs and a long-term financial health plan."

"That sounds promising. But what will we do in the meantime?"

"Pray! And get the word out to the congregation that we need some extra-mile giving. I'll check with one of our members about a short-term loan to get us through the next few months. With God's help, we'll figure this out!"

Healthy, Spirit-led leaders are able to help congregations understand the importance of practicing stewardship and facing their fiscal challenges. They are also able to recognize and draw on the significant resources that are usually already available within the congregation.

This is the sixth transformational key. *A congregation that wants to move forward in mission will find it necessary to practice stewardship as it builds financial viability.*

We've discovered that this is the key that is often missing as congregational leaders look to move a congregation forward on its missional journey. Practicing stewardship toward building financial viability is an issue that, if not taken seriously, can become a huge obstacle to a congregation seeking to implement a missional plan. Financial challenges can also become a flash point for congregational conflict.

One congregation was so convinced that the arrival of their new pastor would be the panacea to all their problems—financial and otherwise—that they passed a budget with a large deficit. "Attendance and giving will automatically go up now that we have a full-time pastor," they reasoned. But by failing to take any specific steps or to make changes to ensure that this would happen, the congregation was doomed to repeat the failed budgets of previous years. "Doing the same thing over and over again and expecting different results" is one definition of insanity.

A Biblical Understanding of Stewardship

One of the foundational truths taught in the Bible is the importance of good stewardship. Seminary professor Rolf Jacobson notes, "In the ancient world, the word steward . . . describes a person—normally a slave—who was placed in a position of responsibility over the property, possessions, or household of another person, to whom the household actually belonged. The concept thus offers promise as a model for Christian congregational identity."[1]

Think of us this way, as servants of Christ
and stewards of God's mysteries.
Moreover, it is required of stewards
that they be found trustworthy.
(1 Cor. 4:1-2)

As discussed in chapter two, God the Creator desires to be reconciled with all of creation lost in the fall—everyone, everywhere, and everything. God the Spirit creates congregations as the primary agents for carrying out this ministry of reconciliation: "in Christ God was reconciling the world to himself . . . and entrusting the message of reconciliation to us. So we are ambassadors for Christ" (2 Cor 5:19-20a).

Congregations stand at the center of God's redemptive work in the world. They are to enact the reality of redemption in all of life within their own ministry and participate in God's mission in the world as agents of reconciliation within the larger community they seek to serve. This is the biblical understanding of a servant ministry of stewardship—being "servants of Christ and stewards of the mysteries of God." As Rolf Jacobson points out, this has a number of important implications for understanding congregational identity, *all of which also deeply inform the stewarding of finances within congregational life.* The following points are adapted from Jacobson's argument.[2]

- *God's mission and the means to sustain it belong to God.* The Scripture teaches that our worldly possessions are given to us by God, and that we are responsible for stewarding them well for the purpose of participating in God's mission in the world.
- *Congregations are corporate communities that steward God's mission in a particular place and time.* The primary responsibility of a congregation is to be a faithful steward of God's mysteries by bearing witness to the kingdom of God within the larger community regard-

ing the fullness of redemption available from God. Congregations must take the needs of their local community seriously when considering the stewardship of their resources.

- *To join a congregation is to respond to God's call to join in God's mission as a steward.* This means that congregations consist, not of members with rights and privileges, but rather of disciples who live out the full meaning of the gospel. Congregations are to do this as a community that is both gathered to nurture is own life and sent into its larger community to serve the needs of others.

- *Stewards are expected to be trustworthy as well as accountable.* How a congregation as a community stewards its corporate life, which includes the stewarding of the financial resources available to them, is foundational to being honored by God as a trustworthy and accountable steward.

Stewardship is not optional nor is it just one more thing disciples are responsible to engage in. Rather, stewardship stands at the very center of Christian identity, both for congregations as communities and for individual Christians as disciples of Jesus. It is this understanding that needs to serve as the foundation for helping congregations develop financial viability.

Is the Glass Half Full or Half Empty?

It is helpful to understand the history of giving in a particular congregation. A healthy, Spirit-led leadership team will start by taking the financial temperature of a congregation. Congregational leaders can ascertain what might be the *regular* pattern of giving by member units by asking several questions. How many members make an annual pledge to the church's budget? How many contribute something on a weekly or monthly basis? How many are committed to percentage giving? How do your members compare with the national average?

It is interesting to note that in 2005 the average charitable giving for church attendees was $1,232; and the average gift of those who identified themselves as Evangelical Christians was $3,250.[3] Another significant finding, from research done by the Gallup organization in

2005, is that active, engaged members give a median of 5 percent of their annual household incomes to their church. That is nearly twice as much as the not-so-engaged, who gave on average about 3 percent.[4] While it doesn't take much thought to put a ten- or twenty-dollar bill into the offering plate, most families have to think seriously about giving a regular percentage of their household income to the church—especially when faced with many other financial obligations including food, housing, health care, college and retirement funds, credit card debt, car payments, and insurance. Often these competing obligations lead people to believe their resources are scarce and that they don't have enough money to give to the church.

In addition to ascertaining congregational giving patterns, it is important to understand how a congregation perceives its financial situation. Many congregations see themselves as asset poor, lacking any real knowledge about the financial abilities of congregational members or the church's resources. Even though we live in the richest nation on the planet, many congregations, regardless of their actual resources, embrace an attitude of scarcity rather than of abundance. When faced with financial challenges, many are apt to throw up their hands in a hopeless gesture, claiming they have no idea where additional funds might be found to fund ministry and cannot perceive it otherwise. For them the glass is always half empty.

Healthy, Spirit-led leaders help congregations do a reality check. By doing a little research into the financial demographics of congregational members and the people whom the church serves, and then by educating members about what is learned, it may be possible to help the congregation realize that the glass is really half full! The congregation may discover that they have more financial resources at their disposal than they could possibly have imagined.

Mapping Assets: Taking Stock of Resources

There's a story about a pastor who, after a tornado had damaged the church building, got up before his congregation on a Sunday morning and announced: "Friends, I have some bad news and some good news.

The bad news is that the building contractor has told us that it will cost $250,000 to replace our church roof. The good news is that we already have all the money we need." An excited buzz rippled through the congregation. "There's only one problem," the pastor continued. "The money is still in our pockets!"

Nurturing an attitude of abundance begins by considering one's image of God. In his second letter to the Corinthians, Saint Paul indicates that a believer's generosity is both inspired and surpassed by God's grace. He encourages members of the early Christian community to contribute to the needs of the church's ministry, and reminds them that "God is able to provide you with every blessing in abundance, so that by always having enough of everything, you may share abundantly in every good work" (2 Cor. 9:8).

Asset mapping is a tool to help the congregation name the resources and gifts with which they have been blessed—both corporately and individually. It involves leaders making a list of the congregation's tangible and intangible assets. Tangible assets include such things as money in the bank, the value of church property, educational materials, and music resources (handbells, choir music, and the like). Intangible resources include the skills and talents of church staff and members. Conducting a spiritual gifts inventory for members is helpful in identifying intangible assets that are so important for ministry. Lest we forget, one of the spiritual gifts listed in the New Testament is that of *giving generously*!

The Pastor as Fund Raiser

Since giving is a spiritual issue that reflects one's relationship with God, who is better qualified to speak on this matter than the pastor? Many pastors shy away from addressing money issues, other than preaching the obligatory annual stewardship sermon, perhaps forgetting that Jesus talked a great deal about money. Sixteen of Jesus' thirty-eight parables are concerned with money and possessions. An amazing one out of ten verses in the Gospels (288 in all) deal directly with the subject of money. The Bible offers 500 verses on prayer, fewer than 500 verses on faith, yet more than 2,000 verses on money and possessions. It seems that Jesus realized that one's attitude toward possessions was indeed a spiritual matter and needed to be taken seriously.

The new pastor spoke very bluntly in his sermon about the unhealthy financial situation facing Amazing Grace. He challenged members to look into their own hearts, and their pocketbooks, to consider how they would respond to the situation. He reminded parishioners that their checkbooks reflected their priorities and the nature of their discipleship. He concluded, "All things belong to God and we are but the managers of God's gifts and blessings. If all of life is to be understood as stewardship, then we will be accountable to God for how we make use of the things that have been entrusted into our care."

As members departed the church after worship, many stopped at the door to thank the pastor for being so honest. One longtime member summed up the sentiment of most worshipers that day: "You're the first pastor who has spoken openly and truthfully about finances."

Perhaps your pastoral staff has administrative or accounting skills that can be useful in helping congregations build financial stability. If not, it will be important that they seek out individuals who do, and invite them to help steward the congregation financially, consulting with them on a monthly basis. Pastors would do well to take time to be acquainted with the congregation's spending for its missional plan, be aware of the kind of progress the congregation is making toward its financial goals during the course of the year, and make sure that the congregation's leaders stay informed.

Amazing Grace developed a simple but informative financial report that can serve as a helpful tool in monitoring financial progress, and is easily adaptable to most any size congregation (see appendix B, page 141). It won't be necessary for congregational leaders to spend an inordinate amount of time at council or ministry team meetings discussing finances if they know that key leaders, including the pastor, are aware of and transparent about the financial state of the parish, and that appropriate steps are being taken to ensure that the mission plan of the congregation will be funded.

Some Strategies for Financial Health

There are several strategies that can help a congregation advance down the road to financial recovery and stability. One best practice followed by businesses that plan strategically for wise use of financial resources is a "*Grow, Hold, and Fold*" analysis. The following questions help leaders determine what a congregation can relinquish in order to have the resources to grow certain ministry areas.

- Where do we invest our gifts (human and financial) for growth for the future?
- What do we sustain for the future at approximately the same level we do now?
- What do we stop doing so that we may focus resources on our "grow" and our "hold" opportunities?

Although many congregations have a finance committee that monitors congregational spending, it is sometimes necessary to call together a special team of trusted financial advisors. This team is often appointed rather than elected. They are pillars of the church, usually with deep pockets, who have demonstrated good business sense in their professions. In the case study that opened this chapter, the pastor and council president assembled such a team. They asked for help not only in addressing an immediate financial crisis, but also in coming up with a strategy to ensure long-term financial viability for the congregation. In the case of Amazing Grace, this team offered a threefold strategy:

- Obtain a short-term loan from a member to take care of current financial obligations.
- Encourage members to make a 25 percent increase in their annual commitment in support of the congregation's budget.
- Hold a debt-reduction campaign that would free up money in the annual budget for ministry by reducing monthly mortgage payments.

This last strategy is born out of the adage that "money follows vision." Both staff and lay leaders must be clear about articulating the purpose and vision of the congregation. Requests for funding always need to be connected with the missional plan. Leaders should be able to point out how members are helping accomplish the congregation's vision for ministry. In addition to encouraging regular giving to support the general ministry of the parish, it's wise to discover what people are passionate about and then invite them to participate in a specific way by sharing both their talents and their financial resources. One might consider using the following survey to ascertain what people might also support.

Sharing in God's Mission: A Personal Response

1. The congregation is thriving five years from now. What happened? List three changes or innovations that helped move the congregation forward in mission.

2. What are the things you are passionate about regarding God's work through our congregation?

3. What are the resources that you could offer to help us accomplish this?

How a church builds a stable financial base for mission and ministry is a critical question every leadership team must grapple with if a congregation is to be successful in accomplishing its missional objectives. Establishing good stewardship practices is one of the first steps in answering this question. Healthy, Spirit-led leaders will lead by example in this ministry of generosity, thus setting the tone for a faithful response by God's people.

Discovery Questions

1. How does the Bible teach us about stewardship? How does this inform a congregation's identity?

2. In what ways is financial health a sign of congregational vitality and commitment to participation in God's mission? Why is financial viability important for a congregation to accomplish its missional plan?

3. How does building passion for God's mission relate to the development of broad ownership of a congregation's missional plan?

4. It has often been said that money follows vision. To what extent do you feel this is true? Explain.

Resources for the Journey

Bacher, Robert and Michael Cooper-White. *Church Administration: Programs, Process, Purpose.* Minneapolis: Augsburg Fortress, 2007.

Hudnut-Beumler, James. *Generous Saints: Congregations Rethinking Ethics and Money.* Herndon, Va.: Alban Institute, 1999.

Jacobson, Rolf. "Stewards of God's Mysteries: Stewarding as a Model for Congregational Ministry," in *Word & World* 26, no. 3 (Summer 2006): 249–258.

Lane, Charles. *Ask, Thank, Tell: Improving Stewardship Ministry in Your Congregation.* Minneapolis: Augsburg Books, 2006.

Minatrea, Milfred. *Shaped by God's Heart: The Passion and Practices of Missional Churches.* San Francisco: Jossey-Bass, 2004.

O'Hurley-Pitts, Michael. *The Passionate Steward.* New York: St. Brigid, 2002.

Celebrate Successes and the Contributions of All

Amazing Grace Church had just completed a successful debt reduction campaign. At worship on Sunday morning, the chair of the campaign got up to announce the results. He strode over to the microphone with a spring in his step and commended the congregation for stepping up to the plate and exceeding the goal.

Then he added, "There is one person who deserves much of the credit for the success of the campaign. He worked many hours to help us organize and carry out a first-class program. He was tireless in his energy and eager to share his experience and ideas with us. He and his wife also gave a generous gift to the campaign. We owe a great deal of gratitude to our new lead pastor."

The congregation was on its feet with applause. The pastor rose to acknowledge the gesture of appreciation. He motioned for people to be seated and then shared his thoughts.

"Thank you for your affirmation," the pastor began. "While Ron is very generous in his comments, there is no way that I can take the credit for the success of this campaign. It was a team effort as is everything here at Amazing Grace. None of us can accomplish much by ourselves, but, as we've seen today, together we can do great things."

The pastor paused for a moment before adding, "There were many people, including the wonderful staff of Amazing Grace, who worked hard behind the scenes. We also had a great campaign team that needs to be thanked. I would like everyone who helped in any way to stand up and be recognized."

Servant leaders accept words of appreciation while recognizing that celebrating success it is not about them, but about lifting up the whole people of God.

This is the seventh transformational key.
It is important to celebrate our successes along the way and, especially, the accomplishments of others.

We are nearing the end of our quest to become missional congregations. Like all good explorers, you will want to revisit the practices we've discussed so far to see how they are being lived out in the life of your congregation. When doing so, please keep in mind that none of these transformational keys are intended to be the *solution* in and of themselves. Rather, they are markers along the journey of leading congregations successfully through change and transition toward engaging more fully in God's mission in the world. Before we're done, however, there is one more transformational key to be examined.

Change Is Normal

It is critical to understand that change in the life of a congregation and the larger community it serves is *normal*. Chapter two discussed the importance of understanding the humanness of congregations in the midst of their holiness. This humanness brings the larger community into play as one aspect of a congregation's identity. It is helpful, therefore, for congregations to take steps to stay aware of the ongoing changes associated with its context. Such changes often necessitate making changes in the approach to a congregation's ministry, and these changes, as noted in chapter seven, can often generate conflict.

Contexts Are Always Changing

Another critical realization is that contexts are always changing. This is certainly the case with Amazing Grace Church. It is crucial for congregations like Amazing Grace to anticipate change and plan how to continually reconnect ministry to changing conditions, so as to participate more fully in God's mission. Unfortunately, this doesn't happen often enough. We saw that Amazing Grace had become out of step with the larger community. Getting back in step involves understanding that changes in a particular congregational context can vary in both scope and speed.

Some Contexts Change Incrementally Over Time

Until recent decades, change in the context of most congregations was usually incremental, being experienced over extended periods of time.

The stable makeup of the neighborhood population around Amazing Grace in the 1960s and 1970s allowed for substantial continuity in the congregation's ministry patterns and organizational forms. But while Amazing Grace was able to function for long periods of time with relative stability, the cumulative effects of incremental change finally caught up with the congregation. Amazing Grace saw the aging of most of the longer-term, Anglo residents of their community, and the subsequent decline in the number of children in the congregation.

Some Contexts Change Dramatically

There are times in the life of the church when change occurs in a tumultuous manner that interrupts the status quo. This is referred to as discontinuous change, a type of change that has become much more common in recent decades. This introduces a situation where there are no clear ways to predict how to move forward based on previous experience.[1]

This type of change has increasingly becoming the case for Amazing Grace, at least in relation to both apartment dwellers and the Hispanic residents who now reside in the neighborhood. Such change usually brings substantial disruption to the life of congregations. Typically, there is a delayed response to this type of change. While there may be early indications that changes are occurring, few congregations are prepared to read these signs in time to implement effective strategies to respond. This was the case for Amazing Grace Church, which had assumed a reactive posture toward change.

Change Can Be Both Helpful and Harmful

There are many cases where contextual changes, although initially disruptive, can actually benefit congregations and their ministries. The migration of persons from other ethnicities into a congregation's broader community, as was the case for Amazing Grace, can actually invite a congregation to develop a missional imagination for serving and reaching out to what we often think of as the other. There are, however, some changes in the context around a congregation that are profoundly difficult to respond to, and may even be harmful. Natural disasters are devastating to the well-being of human life and disruptive to congregational life. Dramatic changes in the local economy brought on by the loss of a major employer can also have devastating effects on a congregation.

Change needs to be assessed carefully to discern whether it is helpful, harmful, or even both. This is a continuous task for a congregation seeking by the power of the Spirit to be faithful in proclaiming the gospel in its particular context. This is especially the case for congregations seeking to reconnect ministry to a changing context. It's important for congregations to develop the internal capacity to respond to such changes without becoming internally conflicted.

The Challenge of Transition and Change

The church, as it seeks to participate in God's mission, is called to be an agent of change in both its larger community and in the world. God uses the church as an instrument of transformation to bring about peace, justice, and salvation. Theologians Norma Cook Everist and

Craig Nessan caution that "The challenges are immense: peace does not rule, justice is fragmentary, people are hungry, violence tears us apart, creation groans. Yet through the work of the Spirit, this transforming God continues to call, equip, and empower [the church] to live boldly in transforming ways."[2] When the church has failed in this respect, it is primarily because it has turned inward; becoming self-serving and preoccupied with its own self-preservation. For this, the community of faith needs to repent and heed the New Testament call to death and resurrection.

The mainline church and its witness are in dire straights. According to David Lose, Professor of Biblical Preaching at Luther Seminary in St. Paul, Minnesota, if things do *not* change, most of us will live to see the end of mainline denominations as we know them. He states: "Unfortunately the reaction to this news is to become self-absorbed with survival and is antithetical to the Gospel message which promises resurrection from the dead. We must look not inward but outward, not to what we need but what the world needs. We must be willing to spend ourselves for the sake of the world that God loves so very much."[3]

A walk through the rain forest in Washington State reveals much about the natural order of God's creation. It also provides a clue to the cycle of life and death in the church. Everything in the forest is interdependent and is part of a larger ecosystem. A nurse log is a good example. Old growth trees that have fallen and decayed become, in their death, a source of new life for young saplings that will one day stand strong and tall. Perhaps this is a sign of hope for congregations—out of death can come new and vibrant life. God's people are being called to die to old paradigms and cease our clinging to the past in order to rise to new life as a missional community of faithful disciples.

The average life span of a vital congregation has been estimated to be forty years, after which a congregation must reinvent itself (find a renewed sense of purpose) if it is to move forward with integrity and new energy into God's missional future. With the current pace of cultural change accelerating, this likely shortens the life cycle even further so that congregations will need to engage in a transformational process every ten to twenty years.

The following diagram outlines the process of change and transformation in the life of a congregation as it seeks to embrace God's missional future. It assumes that a congregation is most open to change after a time of crisis or challenge, so that the first step is to seek stability while becoming grounded in missional principles. Then the congregation can proceed to the tasks necessary for bringing about transformation and a new beginning.

BECOMING A MISSIONAL CONGREGATION
(Movement from In-reach to Outreach)

Phase One: From Transition to Stability	Phase Two: From Stability to Transformation
Healing and rebuilding trust	Manage conflict and build ownership for the vision
Developing vision for a strategic plan	Review and recommit to missional objectives
Nurturing healthy team of staff and leaders	Staff for growth
Providing a stable financial base	Offer a visionary mission spending plan
Rebuilding of ministries	Focus on quality and expansion of ministries (small groups, inspiring worship, youth, etc.)

Change and transition are never easy, especially as one seeks to pursue the Spirit-led transformation of the culture of a congregation. There are two myths that healthy leaders have to face and put to rest:
- The church can grow without changing.
- One can change without conflict.

In her insightful book, *When Better Isn't Enough: Evaluation Tools for the 21st Century Church*, Jill Hudson writes,

> Everything has a cost. We know this in our heart, and yet we try to avoid it. We want the "old" church just as it was, with comforting hymns, informally claimed pews, and familiar liturgies. We also want the benefits of the "new church," full of young families and hope for the future. We want new believers who mature in Christ and share the responsibilities of church membership. We don't want anyone mad—ever! We want it both ways. We want the comfort of the past and the promise of the future without alienating anyone.[4]

Not everyone will be happy with the idea of a changing church for a changing world, and a congregation needs to be prepared for some fallout. It is critical, as we've seen, to vigorously invite everyone to join the journey of being part of the transformational process. This chapter addresses several important principles in leading a congregation successfully through times of change and transition. These include celebrating milestones of progress as a congregation lives into a new reality as a missional church; empowering and then recognizing God's people for their contributions toward helping create a new future; and providing ongoing opportunities for transformation along the way.

Celebrate Milestones of Success

One congregation, which had experienced the loss of their campus to an arson fire, made an intentional decision to celebrate certain milestones along the way of rebuilding the church facilities and their sense of mission. They invited members of the congregation and people from the surrounding community to celebrate their progress as they moved from "death to new life." One occasion was the laying of the cornerstone of the new church. In a gesture of healing and reconciliation, the arsonist's family was asked to participate and was given one of the gold-painted shovels from the service. Several other events were observed along the way, culminating with the dedication of a new sanctuary. The father of the arsonist spoke at the event and through his tears said, "For me this new church building is the symbol of the rebuilding of lives."

It is important to take time during the course of any transition to mark milestones signaling growth and improvement. Sometimes this may be through a special event or a worship service of thanksgiving. Other times it may simply involve reminding the congregation of the progress being made toward accomplishing missional objectives. It can be helpful, for example, for a core leadership team comprised of the pastor and executive officers to review the congregation's missional plan and issue quarterly reports on any movement being made. This can be shared and celebrated at quarterly team meetings and also with the congregation as whole.

Assessment is a Necessary Part of the Process

In order to know when progress has been made and celebration is merited, it is important to take time to evaluate and reflect on how things are going. Various assessment tools can be helpful at different stages of the transformational journey both to measure successes and to benchmark current conditions in the congregation in order to determine the congregation's readiness for the next steps. Such assessment can help a leadership team decide how to prioritize and where to allocate resources for the coming year.

One helpful tool is the *Natural Church Development* survey (see www.ncdnet.org). This measures eight qualities of congregational vitality including empowering leadership, gift-oriented ministry, passionate spirituality, functional structures, inspiring worship, holistic small groups, need-oriented evangelism, and loving relationships. Another assessment instrument prepared by the Hartford Institute for Religious Research is the *Church Planning Inventory and Parish Profile Inventory* that is available online at www.hirr.hartsem.edu. Likewise The Alban Institute (www.alban.org) has helpful resources. Also worth looking at is the new Transforming Church Network, which provides a church assessment tool along with professional church consultation.

Their Web site can be found at www.transformingchurch.net. We also encourage leaders to check with their denomination to see what other evaluation tools may be available. Often a quick review of a denomination's Web site will unearth resources that are free and readily available, but not widely publicized.

The Power of Affirming Others

The power of affirmation cannot be underestimated. As leaders seek to empower all of God's people to use their gifts in service, it is equally important to recognize the contributions that individuals make by their participation in God's mission through the church and in the community. The task of a missional church in unleashing the gifts of God's people is threefold: 1) assist people in discovering their passion and gifts, 2) help them assume greater ownership of the congregation's life and purpose, and 3) affirm their ministry in daily life. Pastor Rick Barger offers the reminder that "Discipleship is not to exhaust people or fragment families because they spend too much time doing 'church work.' Discipleship is putting one's passions to work in ways that promote wellness and wholeness in the whole of life and in all arenas, in the church and the world, for the sake of Jesus."[5]

People appreciate being recognized. Organizations that depend on volunteers who selflessly share their time, energy, and resources know the importance of acknowledging the contributions of the committed leaders and participants who make things happen. Some churches are better at acknowledging such contributions than others. We offer as example a congregation that hosts a Sunday brunch each year to celebrate faithful volunteers. Another congregation in a retirement community holds a special midweek luncheon program where certificates of recognition are handed out. Other congregations have a regular "Thanks to You!" column in the congregational newsletter that acknowledges those who help out in that month. Others recognize special "volunteers of the quarter."

Worship is a good time to affirm people in various ministries, especially as they begin a task. A brief commissioning service for church council members or Sunday school and preschool teachers is a way of lifting up those called to a particular service before the whole church. Some congregations designate one Sunday a month to recognize various professions (such as those in health care, education, etc.) as a means of affirming members living out their faith in their daily life.

People are motivated by more than just monetary rewards. Most are grateful to be recognized for their gifts and contributions. This affirmation encourages them to continue their service and to become even more supportive of the congregation's mission. If people feel appreciated, they often will be motivated to give more of their time, talent, and treasure to a cause they feel passionate about.

A longtime church worker reflected at a staff retreat on the climate change that had taken place among the staff of Amazing Grace. "We used to come to the occasional staff meeting and feel the tension in the room," she said. "Now it is a joy to come to work because everyone is so supportive and encouraging of each other." Everyone else agreed that this was the result, in part, of leaders nurturing a culture of appreciation among both staff and members.

Such a culture is not accidental. It is built by attending to relationships, and showing others respect, affection, and admiration.[6]

Share Transforming Experiences

Transformation begins with a group of healthy leaders who are committed to change. A famous anthropologist, Margaret Meade, said, "Never doubt that a group of small, thoughtful citizens can change the world; indeed it is the only thing that ever has."[7] Often change takes place as leaders invite people to join with them in experiences that can lead to transformation. Consider the following story.

Amazing Grace Church continued to embrace its outward calling to serve the wider world in a variety of ways. One involved a decision to serve as a sponsor of a new Hispanic mission congregation in their community. When the pastor of Amazing Grace Church was invited to come and preach to this recently formed congregation, a small delegation went with him—partly out of curiosity but also to show their support. While the worship service was mostly in Spanish, both the pastor and church president of the Hispanic mission shared greetings in English, sharing their deep appreciation for this new partnership in the gospel. Following worship, everyone gathered in the fellowship hall for a traditional Posada, a special celebration meal. Youth of the congregation who were proficient in English sat with their guests from Amazing Grace, exhibiting first-rate hospitality. The experience had a profound effect on members of the delegation.

A few days later, one of the older members of Amazing Grace who had attended the event at the Hispanic mission spoke with his pastor. "I used to drive by the local Home Depot," he said, "and wonder why all those men didn't just go back across the border. But I don't anymore." He paused and then continued, "I realize they are fellow believers just like us with families to support, and who have hopes and dreams of a better tomorrow."

Changing the world often takes place one person at a time. "Cherish yesterday, dream tomorrow, and live today" could well be the motto of a congregation willing to take the journey of transformation to becoming a missional church. Leaders do well to lift up and celebrate the rich history and legacy of their congregation while inviting their fellow members to live into God's new future. While dreaming and planning to be part of God's missional future, the people of God need to live fully in the moment, embracing God's gracious call to serve fully in the present, and celebrating all that God's Spirit is doing in our midst even now.

 ## Discovery Questions

1. How should congregations understand and respond to change taking place both within their own life and in

their larger community? What changes are taking place in your congregation and community? How are you responding?

2. Why is it important to celebrate achievement milestones? How do such celebrations relate to gaining a better understanding of the presence and work of God's Spirit in a congregation's life and ministry?

3. How does your congregation show appreciation to its members and staff? How well do you say "thank you"?

4. As you think about your congregation, how many people typically receive public acknowledgement or receive public credit for their contributions to various ministries? Why is it important to acknowledge the contributions and gifts of all God's people?

5. To what extent does your congregation recognize the accomplishments of those who do ministry outside of the church in the larger community? To what extent does your congregation understand this to be part of its fuller participation in God's mission in the world?

Resources for the Journey

Bacher, Robert and Kenneth Inskeep. *Chasing Down a Rumor: The Death of Mainline Denominations.* Minneapolis: Augsburg Books, 2005.

Barger, Rick. *A New and Right Spirit: Creating an Authentic Church in a Consumer Culture.* Herndon, Va.: Alban Institute, 2005.

Ford, Kevin. *Transforming Church: Bring Out the Good to Get to Great.* Carol Stream, Ill.: Tyndale House, 2007.

Frambach, Nathan. *Emerging Ministry: Being Church Today.* Minneapolis: Augsburg Fortress, 2007.

Hudson, Jill. *When Better Isn't Enough: Evaluation Tools for the 21st Century.* Herndon, Va.: Alban Institute, 2007.

Lewis, Robert and Wayne Cordeiro. *Culture Shift: Transforming Your Church from the Inside Out.* San Francisco: Jossey-Bass, 2005.

Nadler, David A., Robert B. Shaw, A. Elise Walton and associates. *Discontinuous Change: Leading Organizational Transformation.* San Francisco: Jossey-Bass, 1994.

Epilogue

The Missional Journey: Bearing Witness to the Kingdom of God

This book has regularly made reference to God's mission in the world, and the responsibility of the church to participate more fully in it. This is what we believe is the quest of a missional congregation, a quest that we have invited your congregation to pursue as a journey of transformation. We have regularly stressed the importance of the missional congregation seeking to discern the leading of the Spirit both in the life of a congregation and, through the congregation, in the larger community. We've argued that the primary responsibility of congregational leaders is to steward the mysteries of God in the ministry of the congregation. They are to help all members, in light of their baptism, to corporately and individually live out their vocation in the world.

It is critical to remember that the world is always the larger horizon for the missional congregation. This is why we have stressed over and over the importance of congregations being intentional about getting to know and then engage the communities within which they are located. Interestingly, the Bible uses the image of the kingdom of God as a primary way for cultivating an imagination for defining the relationship of a congregation to its larger context. The key to understanding the kingdom of God is to explore carefully how God's intent for all of creation was embodied in the life of Jesus and was announced in his ministry. Summarized below are a few final reflections on the responsibility of the missional congregation to continuously bear witness to God's kingdom.

Missional Theology and the Kingdom of God

Congregations are marked with the cross of Christ forever. The death and resurrection of Jesus stands at the center of a congregation's identity. The ascended Jesus, now seated at the right hand of God, still bears fully the marks of the cross in his resurrected body. Jesus taught his followers about the necessity of his death and resurrection as being the key to understanding God's ministry of reconciliation within all of life and throughout all the world. In trying to help his followers understand this, Jesus connected God's work of reconciliation to his teaching about the kingdom of God.

Jesus organizes his teaching in the Gospel accounts around the kingdom of God. In the Gospels, we learn that God's kingdom is present in our midst: "the kingdom of God is among you" (Luke 17:21). It is to be received (Mark 10:15). People are invited to seek it (Matt. 6:33) and to enter into it (Matt. 23:13). They also look toward that day when they will inherit it (Matt. 25:34). The coming of the kingdom is about the power of God's love and grace confronting and defeating the power of the enemy, the evil one (Matt. 4:1-11).

Living in the kingdom, in the redemptive reign of God in Christ, illnesses are healed (Matt. 11:4-5), evil spirits are cast out (Mark 1:39), and natural circumstances are changed (Mark 6:47-52), even as the poor hear the gospel of the kingdom as good news (Luke 4:18-19). Jesus uses parables to explain the kingdom as a mystery that only some have ears to hear and eyes to see (Matt. 13:10-17). The Father gives the kingdom as a gift to the followers of Jesus, and accepting this gift radically changes the way one looks at material possessions (Luke 12:32-34). While the presence and influence of God's kingdom will grow dramatically in the world (Matt. 13:31-32), there are many who think they are part of God's kingdom who will miss it (Matt. 21:33-44).

Jesus announced that the kingdom was *at hand*, and that redemption would now be brought to bear on all of life. To that end, Jesus invited *everyone, everywhere* to repent and believe this good news (Mark 1:14-15). To spread this message, Jesus gathered followers who would learn to "fish for people" (Mark 1:17), and would serve as the foundation of the church that Jesus would himself build: "I will build my church" (Matt. 16:18). Anticipating his death, Jesus prayed not only for his followers, but also for all who would come to believe in him through their testimony (John 17:20).

Following his death and resurrection, Jesus made it clear that his followers were to take the message of salvation and reconciliation, rooted in God's kingdom, which is the redemptive reign of God in Christ, to all people and to the ends of the earth—to *everyone, everywhere*—and bear witness to its truths in relation to all of life and *everything* (Matt. 28:19-20; Luke 24:47). Jesus also conveyed to his followers that God would send the Spirit to lead them in this work and empowered them to carry it out (Luke 24:49; John 14:25-26; John 20:22). Jesus clearly anticipated that a movement, persons later identified as Christians (Acts 11:26), as well as a new type of organization, the church as a called-out community, would grow from the witness of his followers under the inspiration of the Spirit (Matt. 16:18; John 17:20). This new community we understand to be the *missional congregation*.

A Quest that Becomes a Journey

We believe that missional congregations should seek to be led by the Spirit in taking a journey of spiritual transformation that shapes their lives and informs their ministries. We have discussed this as a quest that becomes a journey. Our prayer is that you and your congregation will, indeed, engage the quest and enjoy the journey.

Appendix A

Amazing Grace Church Strategic Plan

Our History

Founded in 1956, Amazing Grace was from its inception a leading congregation in the South Pacific District of the American Lutheran Church (now ELCA). The congregation has helped to launch numerous new mission starts, has sponsored missionaries overseas, and is active in local community service projects.. The congregation has always had a commitment to excellence in worship, music, and the arts. The church's Kids Academy serves 200 children a day (preschool through kindergarten), and over fifty elementary and middle school children in an after-school program of music and the arts.

Our Values

Faith

We endeavor to help members and others grow in their Christian faith and daily spiritual walk.

Service

We are dedicated to living out the gospel by serving one another and neighbors in need.

Community

We seek to help build a sense of acceptance and belonging among all members and friends of the congregation.

Mutual Support

We seek to foster a spirit of cooperation and collegiality, recognizing that we accomplish our best when we are connected, supportive, and interdependent with one another.

Trust

We foster a climate of mutual respect and trust among staff, leaders, and members.

Empowerment

We desire to be a place of learning for all ages and to equip and empower people to use their gifts and discover their passion in order to more effectively carry out their ministry in the church and in the world.

Mission Outreach

We are committed to living out the Great Commission (making disciples) and believe that our lay members are the "front line missionaries" sharing the good news in the world.

Excellence

We believe that anything worth doing is worth doing well to the glory of God.

Lutheran Tradition

We value our Lutheran heritage and a ministry grounded in Word and Sacrament.

Commitment

> *We strive to live out our commitment to God, the church, and each other by using our gifts and talents to promote the gospel of Jesus Christ.*

Our Purpose

> *Healing hurts, renewing hope, rebuilding dreams.*

Our Vision

> *To be a spiritual fitness center—a place for nurturing modern day disciples of Jesus in their spiritual journey and a center for equipping all people to live out their faith in their daily life and ministry.*

Our Short-Term Strategic Goals (1–2 years)

1. *Provide a solid financial base for the congregation's ministry by refinancing the church mortgage and nurturing passionate stewardship among congregation members.*
2. *Assist members in identifying their gifts and passion for ministry—both within and outside the congregation.*
3. *Strengthen the Christian education program for all ages (including Sunday school and adult offerings on Sundays and weekdays).*
4. *Build a dynamic youth and young adult ministry (including high school and college-age youth), expand the confirmation program to include sixth- through ninth-grade youth, and involve all children and youth in inspiring programs of music and other arts.*
5. *Implement a contemporary worship service by adding a second Sunday worship service by fall.*

Our Long-Term Strategic Goals (3–5 years)

1. *Explore strategies for reaching and retaining young couples and singles in their twenties and thirties (sports league, marriage enrichment, parenting groups, etc.).*

2. *Develop a prayer and healing ministry (prayer team, prayer and healing services, resources on prayer, etc.).*
3. *Offer transformational mission opportunities to members (e.g., mission trips and study seminars outside the United States).*
4. *Expand opportunities for sharing the gospel in our community through a variety of media (podcasts on congregation Web site, radio, cable television, video of worship services, etc.).*
5. *Reactivate the Stephen Ministry program to equip lay caregivers as part of our outreach ministry to people in crisis (health issues, homebound, death of a loved one, etc.) both within and outside the congregation.*

Appendix B

Example Financial Report for Amazing Grace Church

Amazing Grace Church

INCOME STATEMENT	For the Month of October 2007		Compared to a Year Ago		
	Budget	Actual	Last Year		Variance
Envelope	$37,860	$39,257	$34,280	115%	$4,977
Loose	$1,520	$1,035	$748	138.4%	$287
Total Offerings	$39,380	$40,292	$35,028	115.0%	$5,264
Other Receipts					
Special Offerings	$2,500	$2,418	$1,780		$638
Kid's Academy	$5,083	$5,083	$5,083		$0
Other	$5,000	$4,514	$3,840		$674
Total Other Receipts	$12,583	$12,015	$10,703		$1,312
Total Receipts	$51,963	$52,307	$45,731	114%	$6,576

INCOME STATEMENT	For the Ten Months Ended 10/31/07		Compared to a Year Ago		
	Budget	Actual	Last Year		Variance
Envelope	$350,000	$367,258	$321,586	114.2%	$45,672
Loose	$15,000	$17,831	$11,396	156.5%	$6,435
Total Offerings	$365,000	$385,089	$332,982	115.6%	$52,107
Other Receipts					
Special Offerings	$18,000	$11,415	$11,073		$342
Kid's Academy	$40,667	$40,667	$40,667		$0
Other	$75,380	$78,365	$18,635		$59,730
Total Other Receipts	$134,047	$130,447	$70,375		$60,072
Total Receipts	$499,047	$515,536	$403,357	128%	$112,179

Year to Date Expenses	10/31/07		10/31/06		
	Budget	Actual	Actual		Variance
Church Council	$ 1,000	$ 875	$ 1,276	69%	$ (401)
Social Action	$ 8,000	$ 6,875	$ 2,563	268%	$ 4,312
Benevolence	$ 40,000	$ 43,258	$ 27,627	157%	$ 15,631
Outreach	$ 8,000	$ 7,365	$ 8,365	88%	$ (1,000)
Youth and Family Ministry	$ 14,300	$ 12,983	$ 12,151	107%	$ 832
Stewardship	$ 2,000	$ 1,985	$ 685	290%	$ 1,300
Worship	$ 12,000	$ 14,747	$ 3,922	376%	$ 10,825
Discipleship / Small Groups	$ 6,000	$ 5,714	$ 3,696	155%	$ 2,018
Operations	$ 83,025	$ 80,876	$ 69,442	116%	$ 11,434
Administration	$ 41,225	$ 40,040	$ 30,258	132%	$ 9,782
Long-Term Debt	$ 56,275	$ 56,280	$ 57,258	98%	$ (978)
Pastor	$ 65,000	$ 63,785	$ 60,014	106%	$ 3,771
Associate Pastor	$ 6,825	$ 7,015	$ 8,774	80%	$ (1,759)
Pastoral Care	$ 1,500	$ 1,881	$ 1,750	107%	$ 131
Staff Compensation	$ 137,385	$ 136,582	$ 109,675	125%	$ 26,907
Total Expenses	$ 482,535	$ 480,261	$ 397,456	121%	$ 82,805
Net income (Loss)	$ 16,512	$ 35,275	$ 5,901	598%	$ 29,374

Notes

Introduction

1. *Evangelical Lutheran Worship* (Minneapolis: Augsburg Fortress, 2007), 304.

Chapter 1 Does the Church Have a Future?

1. Steven Best and Douglas Kellner, *The Postmodern Turn* (New York: Guilford, 1997).

2. Albert Winseman, *Growing an Engaged Church* (New York: Gallup, 2007), 3.

3. Source: ELCA Research and Evaluation, Trend Report for 1999-2005.

4. Loren B. Meade, *The Once and Future Church: Reinventing the Congregation for a New Mission Frontier* (Herndon, Va.: Alban Institute, 1991).

5. Kenneth W. Inskeep and Daniel S. Taylor, Report on 2006 ELCA Congregation Survey, September 14, 2007.

6. Reggie McNeal, *The Present Future: Six Tough Questions for the Church* (San Francisco: Jossey-Bass, 2003). The categories are McNeal's, but the commentary is specific to this book.

7. ELCA Research and Evaluation, Trend Report for 1999–2005.

8. Matthew 28:18.

9. Rick Rusaw and Eric Swanson, *The Externally Focused Church* (Loveland, Colo.: Group, 2004), 12.

10. Information about the Gospel and Our Culture Network is available at www.gocn.org/main.cfm (accessed August 29, 2007).

11. This is the argument developed in *Missional Church: A Vision for the Sending of the Church in North America*, Darrell L. Guder, ed. (Grand Rapids, Mich.: Eerdmans, 1998).

Chapter 3   Develop a Vision for God's Mission

1. Dave Daubert, *Living Lutheran: Renewing Your Congregation* (Minneapolis: Augsburg Fortress, 2007), 15.

2. Ibid., 38–39.

Chapter 4   Focus on God's Mission and Discipleship

1. Referenced from Loren Meade's book *The Once and Future Church* (Herndon, Va.: Alban Institute, 1990).

2. Edward Hammett and James Pierce, *Reaching People Under 40 While Keeping People Over 60* (St. Louis: Chalice, 2007), 37-43.

3. Craig Nessan, *Beyond Maintenance to Mission* (Minneapolis: Fortress Press, 1999), 55.

4. Jeffrey Jones, *Traveling Together: A Guide for Disciple-forming Congregations* (Herndon, Va.: Alban Institute), pp. 45–46.

5. *Evangelical Lutheran Worship* (Minneapolis: Augsburg Fortress, 2006), 236.

6. Michael Foss, *Power Surge: Six Marks of Discipleship for a Changing Church* (Minneapolis: Fortress Press, 2000), 106.

7. Ibid.

8. Bill Easum, *Leadership on the Other Side: No Rules, Just Clues* (Nashville: Abingdon, 2000), 35.

9. Jones, *Traveling Together*, 134–135.

10. Buechner, Frederick, *Wishful Thinking: A Theological ABC* (New York: Harper, 1982).

Chapter 5   Cultivate a Healthy Climate

1. Norma Cook Everist and Craig Nessan. *Transforming Leadership: New Vision for a Church in Mission* (Minneapolis: Fortress Press, 2008), 40.

2. See Edwin H. Friedman, *Generation to Generation: Family Process in Church and Synagogue* (New York: Guilford, 1985).

3. Israel Galindo, *The Hidden Lives of Congregations: Discerning Church Dynamics* (Herndon, Va.: Alban Institute, 2004), 1.

4. David Laubach, *Twelve Steps to Congregational Transformation: A Practical Guide for Leaders* (Valley Forge, Pa.: Judson, 2006), 27.

5. Ronald A. Heifetz and Marty Linsky, *Leadership on the Line: Staying Alive through the Dangers of Leading* (Boston: Harvard Business School Press, 2002), 14–15.

6. Adapted from *Transforming Leadership*, 40.

7. Peter Steinke, *Healthy Congregations: A Systems Approach* (Herndon, Va.: Alban Institute, 2006).

8. Peter Steinke, *Congregational Leadership in Anxious Times: Being Calm and Courageous No Matter What* (Herndon, Va.: Alban Institute, 2006), 1.

9. Kelly Fryer, *Reclaiming the "C" Word: Daring to Be Church Again* (Minneapolis: Augsburg Fortress, 2006), 46.

10. James Hewett, ed., *Illustrations Unlimited* (Wheaton, Ill.: Tyndale, 1988), 155.

Chapter 6 Build a Supportive Team of Staff and Lay Leadership

1. See Richard Bruesehoff and Phyllis Wiederhoff, *Pastor and People: Making Mutual Ministry Work* (Minneapolis: Augsburg Fortress, 2003), for a good resource for mutual ministry teams. It is important to note that mutual ministry teams do not discipline or make policy. It is the role of the church council and/or personnel committee to hire and fire.

2. Adapted from Norma Cook Everist and Craig Nessan, *Transforming Leadership: New Vision for a Church in Mission* (Minneapolis: Augsburg Fortress, 2008). See page 11.

3. Peter Steinke, *Healthy Congregations Facilitators Manual*, Workshop 3: "Leadership in Healthy Congregations" (Minneapolis: Lutheran Brotherhood, 1999), 49.

Chapter 8   Practice Stewardship to Build Financial Viability

1. Rolf Jacobson, "Stewards of God's Mysteries: Stewarding as a Model for Congregational Ministry," in *Word & World* 26, no. 3 (Summer 2006): 251–252.

2. Ibid., 253–257. Adapted from points developed in Jacobson's essay.

3. The Barna Update, "Americans Donate Billions to Charity, But Giving to Churches Has Declined" (April 25, 2005). For more information check out the Web site for the Barna organization at www.barna.org.

4. Alberet Winseman, *Growing an Engaged Church* (New York: Gallup, 2007), 75.

Chapter 9   Celebrate Successes and the Contributions of All

1. David A. Nadler et al., *Discontinuous Change: Leading Organizational Transformation* (San Francisco: Jossey-Bass, 1994).

2. Norma Cook Everist and Craig Nessan, *Transforming Leadership: New Vision for a Church in Mission* (Minneapolis: Fortress Press), 214.

3. From a presentation by Professor David Lose at the ELCA Worship Jubilee held in Chicago (August 4, 2007).

4. Jill Hudson, *When Better Isn't Enough: Tools for the 21st Century Church* (Herndon, Va.: Alban Institute, 2007), 20.

5. Rick Barger. *A New and Right Spirit: Creating an Authentic Church in a Consumer Culture* (Herndon, Va.: Alban Institute, 2005), 129.

6. *Transforming Leadership*, chapter ten.

7. The Institute for Intercultural Studies, founded by Margaret Meade, does not know an original citation. See their FAQ at www .interculturalstudies.org/faq.html.